GLIMPSES FROM STATE STREET

Smyth & Helwys Publishing, Inc.
6316 Peake Road
Macon, Georgia 31210-3960
1-800-747-3016
©2015 by Wayne Ballard
All rights reserved.

Library of Congress Cataloging-in-Publication Data

Ballard, Wayne, 1963-
Glimpses from State Street / by Wayne Ballard, Jr.
pages cm
Includes bibliographical references and index.
ISBN 978-1-57312-841-4 (pbk. : alk. paper)
1. Meditations. I. Title.
BV4832.3.B35 2015
242--dc23

2015036351

WAYNE BALLARD

- - - -

GLIMPSES

VA *from* TENN

STATE STREET

Also by Wayne Ballard

Exile and Beyond

The Divine Warrior Motif in the Psalms

An Analysis of the Values and Spirituality Profiles of College and University Presidents by Carnegie Classification

A Journey of Faith: An Introduction to Christianity
(with Glenn Jonas, Dean Martin, & Donald Penny)

From Jerusalem to Gaza: An Old Testament Theology
(with B. Donald Keyser)

An Introduction to Wisdom Literature and the Psalms (co-editor)

Dedicated to the Members of the First Baptist Church of
Bristol, Virginia/Tennesee
and
In Memory of
Daniel Steven Hardoby
(March 12, 1949–February 14, 2013)

Acknowledgments

Let me take a moment simply to say thanks to everyone who helped make this book possible. It is always difficult to name individuals because someone ultimately gets left out, and it is *never* my intention to slight anyone.

But I do want to express my appreciation to some of the many people who have helped make my contributions to the church reflected in these brief articles so much easier in these days of transition. The following are in no particular order.

My lovely wife Kim and my sons, Brack and Zachary, tolerated my absence on Sundays and Wednesdays in order for me to serve as the Interim Pastor of the First Baptist Church of Bristol, VA/TN. Thanks to the three of you!

Dr. Gene Eller served faithfully as the pastoral care specialist in the absence of a full-time pastor. He visited the sick, led in the church, and preached numerous funerals over the past nine months. Thank you so much, Gene.

Marilyn Butler was the glue that helped keep the daily operations of the church office together. She is a library of information and did an excellent job in her role as temporary administrative assistant. Marilyn and Beverly Bowers were tremendous encouragers in my writing efforts. In addition to their support on this project, they both helped edit my 2012 dissertation at the University of Tennessee, Knoxville. Thank you so much!

Tom Parker's presence in the area of leadership provided a model of consistency and professionalism that lifted the spirit of everyone he encountered. Tom, thanks for being my friend.

David Hicks did an excellent job as the chairperson of the Deacon Body. In spite of his busy work schedule, David gave of his personal time almost every day for something the church had going on. Mary Beverly also performed admirably, following David as the new chair. Thank you, Mary.

Eric and Angela Hicks and all the music staff did a wonderful job in planning and executing the music ministry of the church. We enjoyed quite a variety of quality music in the fourteen months I was with you!

Joe Emmert made a huge difference every day in the life of the church. As Minister to Families, Joe was busy in many facets of church life and brought great energy to our Sunday morning worship services among the myriad activities that he directed.

Harry Scanlan was a rock of consistency, working with Marilyn to make sure the church office was covered. In addition, he also aided in carrying out pastoral ministry to those in need.

And to all the rest of you, I offer my heartfelt *thank you*. There is not enough room to thank everyone, but I am grateful for you! Some of you were often behind the scenes, but you were invaluable in what you did for our church nonetheless: Chris White, Linda Pruner, Ginny Pullens, Nancy Hyde, Dean Cloyd, Tim Hiss, the Deacon Body, Don Hatcher, Ernie Sprouse, Terri Kiser, Jessica Leonard, and so many more!

Pictures are provided courtesy of Ben Butler, Daniel Hardoby, Believe in Bristol, and Rhythm and Roots. Thanks for sharing your talent for this project.

So let us not grow weary in doing what is right, for we will reap at harvest time, if we do not give up. (Galatians 6:9, NRSV)

Contents

Coming together through Faith

Seasons

Getting Started: An Introduction to Bristol

Ah, the world that is downtown Bristol (Bristol, Virginia, and Bristol, Tennessee)! It is one and the same, and it is a very special place. My story begins on the first Sunday of June 2012, when I began to serve as interim pastor at the First Baptist Church, which is at the end of the downtown stretch of State Street. State Street is a unique area. On the northern side of the yellow line running down the middle of the street is the state of Virginia. On the southern side of the yellow line is the state of Tennessee. The downtown area is filled with restaurants, bars, art galleries, antique merchants, the historic Paramount Theater, and many other interesting shops, coffee stops, and boutiques. An old, historic downtown that was once almost a ghost town has come back to life.

Before you make it to the church, you pass a refurbished train depot that sits beside a large sign hovering over State Street that reads, "Bristol, VA/TENN, A Good Place to Live." From almost any angle, the First Baptist Church is prominently displayed in the background of that large sign and famous landmark. For many people, the only thing known about this iconic place is the Bristol Motor Speedway, which hosts two major NASCAR race events per year. To be quite fair, on these "race weekends," Bristol gladly opens its doors to a couple hundred thousand race fans who contribute significantly to the well-being of this Southern Appalachian economy.

I discovered over the course of fourteen months a city that is welcoming, affirming, and special in the hearts of thousands of its residents and annual visitors. During the year, I had the honor to become intimately acquainted with the city, the people, and the greater area of Bristol.

The purpose of this devotional work is to strengthen you in your day-to-day walk in life. As a Christian minister, I have devoted my life to Christian education, to ministry, and to doing my best to walk in a manner that is worthy to carry the name of Christ. For the past thirty years I have served somewhere almost continuously as a ministerial staff member in Oklahoma, Spain, California, Indiana, Ohio, North Carolina, Tennessee, and Virginia.

These brief devotional readings are the by-product of my years of ministry and are offered to you as words of encouragement and hope. When I first came to serve in Bristol, I was honestly tired and hurting from a previous place of service. A few of my former church members had even become hostile to my family and to me. When you encounter these "dry" times in ministry, you sometimes wonder if you can ever be effective again. In this case, the members of the First Baptist Church were just what my heart and soul needed—a warm cadre of encouragers who faithfully prayed for my family and me each week. With their support, this "interim" time was a very special period in my life.

One of the many blessings of this experience was the expectation that each week I would offer a newsletter article for our church newsletter, "First Word." This was an opportunity for self-expression and a way to offer uplifting words to a body of believers that was also hurting and tired from previous turmoil that had beset the church. Writing these words became a source of therapy and hope for us all. To quote Barney from *The Andy Griffith Show*, "It was *therapetic!*"

Around Christmas 2012, Marilyn Butler, a former instructor of English who was volunteering in the church office, approached me about putting my devotional contributions into a loose-leaf binder and offering them as a fundraiser for a special offering in the church. Each week Marilyn, with the help of Beverly Bowers, Terri Thomas, and Jessica Leonard, spent time editing and "cleaning up" my efforts for weekly publication. When my time as the interim pastor ended, Marilyn presented me with more than a year's worth of weekly encouragements gathered together in a digital format for further use. This devotional book is the final outcome. Though most people could easily read through this material in a short time, I suggest that you read one entry per day. Set the book down and come back later to read another entry. In this manner, I believe you will have more opportunity to realize the purpose for which these words were penned and receive the most benefit from this experience.

Thanks for allowing me the opportunity to share these words with you. Through them, I pray that God will further bless you in your daily walk and draw you closer into an ongoing relationship with God.

Wayne Ballard, Jr.
September 2015

At First Glance

New Beginnings

1

Thank you for the warm welcome this past Sunday morning. It is a true honor to serve the people of First Baptist Church of Bristol as your interim pastor. Moving into a new position is filled with first things: the first Sunday morning service, the first Communion service together, the first newsletter article, the first hospital visit, and on and on and on!

In many ways it is like Opening Day in the Major League Baseball season. My beloved Cleveland Indians are in first place, along with all the other teams of the American League Central Division. This may be the year in my lifetime that the Indians finally win the World Series. There is reason for optimism and hope.

When we get that next full-time pastor, things will be better. We might be able to finally reach the potential that is before us. There is some sense of hope!

But there is a reason that the Cleveland Indians have never won the World Series in my lifetime. It is not because they do not have great players. The success of the New York Yankees over the last century demonstrates how great Indian players have been. Indian greats like Greg Nettles, Chris Chambliss, Ohio native Thurman Munson, C.C. Sabathia, and Bartolo Colon all went on to play for the Yankees and became part of Yankee lore.

So why will the Indians probably not win the World Series again this year? I suggest you consider one part of this problem: tradition (or attitude). The tradition of the New York Yankees is the expectation of winning. Yes, they have some advantages not stated in this brief article, but they expect to win. Most Cleveland fans have become accustomed to losing. There is the expectation that our hearts will be broken once again this year. Indians' fans live under the shroud of Pigpen (of Charlie Brown fame), with the dark cloud of dust hanging over our heads. What can possibly go wrong this year?

When you come to church next Sunday morning, what do you expect to happen? Do you expect to learn something useful in the Sunday school hour? Do you expect God to speak to you in the time of worship? Will you come hoping to respond to God's call in a positive manner this week? What's your expectation for this interim period or for the next full-time pastor who will arrive one day?

I know that the church of Jesus Christ is not a game. If you are thinking we should never relegate church to wins and losses, you are absolutely right. But what church and baseball do have in common is simply this: Do you carry a positive or a negative attitude with you about First Baptist Church of Bristol? People want to come to a church where things are happening. People want to feel God's spirit moving when they open themselves to God to serve in new and exciting ways. Our attitudes determine the words we choose when we describe our church to others. Is it exciting, fresh, inspiring, or hopeful? Or is it dry, staid, declining, or dead?

I encourage you to get into the game. Be involved with the various ministries of the church. Don't grow weary in doing well! Expect great things to happen each week, and don't be shocked when the blessings of God present themselves in our midst. Remember that our attitudes reflect what lies beneath in our hearts and minds. Let people see the love of Jesus Christ in us each week.

No, in all things we are more than conquerors through him who loved us! (Romans 8:37, NIV) The word "conqueror" in this verse comes from two Greek words, *huper nikomen.* And the word *nikomen* comes from the root *nike*, or champion. Paul describes the church as *super champions* or *super winners.* May we live like the champions that God has created us to be.

2

What a Treat

Imagine what appeared this Sunday morning on the shelves of the pastor's office. Church directories from 1984, 1989, 1993, and 1999! I had the best time thumbing through the pages of these "snapshots" from the past two decades of the families at the First Baptist Church of Bristol. It is a joy to be reminded that, even as I look into the mirror, I am not the only one whose appearance has dramatically changed over the course of the past twenty-eight years. Joe Kerr, you know what I mean! What a handsome fellow, especially back in 1984! Some of you have barely changed at all. Most of you are just as handsome or pretty as ever.

As we encounter old directories, we are reminded that years come and go. We, however, are left with a question: What have we done in the time that has been allotted to us? Have we furthered the cause of Christ in the past twenty-eight years? Has the body that is the First Baptist Church been a better place because I have served here? Are there people who have come to a saving knowledge of Jesus Christ because I have cared for them or shared the gospel with them?

We can't change the past. We can change today! What can we do today that will make a difference in someone's life? What can I do that will make a difference in the life of the church? Let me share seven ways we can all make a difference today.

First, all of us can pray. Prayer does change things. Prayer places us in a proper relationship with our Creator. It helps us acknowledge that we don't have to live alone! God is more than ready and willing to guide and direct us each day if we will only lean upon God.

Second, all of us can commit to financially undergirding the ministries of the church through our tithes and offerings. We are at the time of Consecration Sunday, where we pledge our desire to help with the fiscal realities of the church's budget. Have you prayed about what you can do in the upcoming church year?

Third, all of us can share what Jesus Christ has done for us. You have a personal testimony. The most effective witness you have is what God has done for you. It doesn't have to be eloquent or polished. It just has to be honest. When is the last time you shared with a friend what Jesus Christ means to you?

Fourth, all of us can encourage our friends in Christ to continue to grow and serve. Are you helping others draw closer to Christ? Your word of encouragement may mean the difference between someone continuing in the Christian walk, or, if encouragement is not offered, simply walking away from the faith.

Fifth, all of us can commit to making the most of each day in our lives. Are you using the time God has placed before you wisely? We all have the same twenty-four hours to work with each day. Are you managing your time in a way that allows you to celebrate life and have it more abundantly?

Sixth, all of us can laugh more!

Seventh, all of us can care for the needs of our immediate families. Being a committed Christian starts at home. Do your wife, husband, kids, and extended family see the transformation that can only come through a life yielded to Christ? What does your family say about the role your faith plays in your personal life?

If we practice these seven practical tenets, I believe that the directories in 2030 at the First Baptist Church of Bristol will be at least twice as thick as they are now. Let us celebrate the past but plan for a brighter future!

3

Where Are We Going?

Many of you who have received an email from me over the past few months are already acquainted with one of my favorite quotes from a book I read this past year: *"To be a leader, one must both have and embody a vision of where one wants to go. It is not a matter of knowing or believing one is right; it is a matter of taking the first step"* (Edwin H. Friedman, *A Failure of Nerve* [New York: Seabury Books, 2007] 179).

One of my favorite Hollywood blockbusters is the 1951 classic *Quo Vadis*, starring Robert Taylor and Deborah Kerr. Sophia Loren and her mother have brief but un-billed parts in the film. For those of us without a background in Latin, the title simply means "Where are you going?" In this movie, General Marcus Vinicius meets Lygia and falls in love with her when he returns to Rome after a three-year campaign. Lygia is a Christian and doesn't want anything to do with Vinicius since he is a warrior. She is a hostage of Rome, being a princess of a captured people. Vinicius arranges for Emperor Nero to give Lygia to him for services rendered to Rome. Lygia resists but falls in love with him anyway. Nero begins to persecute Christians in Rome severely. When Nero burns Rome and blames the Christians, Vinicius tries to save Lygia and her family. They are all captured and are fated to meet the lions in the coliseum. To learn the fate of Vinicius and Lygia, I suggest you simply watch the movie. It is a good one.

The movie title asks an important question: "Where are you going?" It is a question that we all need to answer from time to time. This past Sunday, the entire church staff gathered on Sunday afternoon to coordinate the ministries for the upcoming calendar year. Of course, dates and activities are all subject to change, but it is going to be an exciting year! I would like to thank our entire staff for their willingness to meticulously go through every week and help put the church calendar together. We are blessed with a wonderful ministry team. I am proud and honored to work with every member of our staff.

In a recent staff meeting, I challenged our church staff to consider three words: *planning, outreach,* and *assessment.* We are well on our way with planning for the upcoming year. Many of the outcomes that we are planning and coordinating have to do with outreach. We can all be part of the outreach ministry of our church, but we need to be intentional with this emphasis. We must invite, call, encourage, and sometimes cajole people to come and experience what we enjoy on a weekly basis at the First Baptist Church of Bristol.

One last word today is "assessment." I shared with our staff my personal belief that we can always improve our work and service. I have encouraged each of them to consider ways that they can assess their work and seek ways to improve. In education today, teachers often fear the word "assessment" because it has been overused and abused in many ways. But assessment can help us personally improve if we take the process seriously and use it in a proper way. I encourage you as a church body to pray for each of our staff members as we plan, reach out, and assess our work in the upcoming church year.

As your interim pastor, I believe that we, the First Baptist Church of Bristol, have begun to take the first step to becoming a healthy and vibrant congregation once again. Is there much work to do? Absolutely. Will it be hard work and sometimes a struggle? Absolutely. But we shall reap a harvest of righteousness if we fail not!

So don't get tired of doing what is good. Don't get discouraged and give up, for we will reap a harvest of blessing at the appropriate time. (Galatians 6:9, NLT)

Quo Vadis?

A Salute to the LLHs of the World

Kim and I had a dear sweet auntie who lived in an exclusive Southern California neighborhood just outside of Dana Point. We used to catch a commuter flight to Ontario and spend the weekend with her when we lived in the Bay Area in Northern California. She was quite the character! She had lived an enchanted life and even ran in the same social group with the Kennedys and the Rothschilds. She had many wonderful expressions that Kim and I still use fondly when remembering her. One of her expressions was to describe cross-country journeys by car as "motoring." When she motored somewhere, it was because she was not in a hurry and simply wanted to travel in a way that she could enjoy the landscape. When I motor somewhere, it usually means I am near broke and cannot afford to fly!

Kim and I have motored all across this great land of ours. We have traveled by car to northeastern Maine and down to San Diego, California. We have driven north from Seattle into western Canada and all the way back to the middle section of Florida. We have seen a lot of interstate driving over our twenty-seven years together.

There is one phenomenon that still drives me nearly insane. I have coined a term to describe drivers who camp out in the left lane and who usually drive just beneath the speed limit, or it describes truckers who think they can pass but wind up spending thirty minutes trying to pass a single vehicle. These people I describe as LLHs—Left Lane Homesteaders.

Even though we often pass traffic posts that read "Slower traffic use right lane," too many drivers simply ignore the law of the land and drive their own way! Granted, there are times when one needs to drive in the left lane only. If there is snow and ice with only one lane cleared, then by all means, use the left lane only. Or, if there are deep grooves in the right lane because of traffic and wear and tear and it is in need of desperate repair, then by all means, use the left lane. But there are too many LLHs who simply don't care about anyone but themselves and stay put in the left lane.

Why the rant this morning? I equate the LLHs of the world with many who are in our society. They know that there is merit to the Christian faith, but they just can't bring themselves to comply with the demands of the call of discipleship. This may include some Christians who have expressed faith in Christ but are still unwilling to fully surrender their own volition. They stop short of following the words of Christ if it means they may have to "drive in the right lane."

Please know that I am not decrying creativity. We can serve Christ in many ways, and following Christ does not demand conformity to the laws of man. But being a Christian does mean that we seek to live like Christ each day. We are to take up our cross daily and follow him. We are to live in such a way that we consider how our actions affect others.

The next time you are driving somewhere and you encounter an LLH, please remember to say a little prayer for that driver and occupants, and examine your own heart to see whether or not you are willing to surrender your will to the will of the Father.

—Your Interim Pastor (Definitely Not a LLH), Wayne Ballard

A Time for Renewal

Wow, time passes by each day. Little by little, life begins to undergo subtle changes right before our eyes. While these changes are taking place, we can also fall into well-worn and rehearsed routines. Some routines are positive, like exercise or mental games. Some routines are less than positive, like too many hours sitting still, or routines involving a favorite flavored coffee or fast food restaurant. Before we know it, we look in the mirror, and we are not the person that we would like to be. Relationships can also become routine or mundane. Even as great as relationships are, if we do not give them ongoing attention, they can become stale and unsatisfying. People we really love and care for may suffer because we have become colder in our hearts, ultimately pushing those we love farther away from us.

This can also happen in our church or in our relationship with Christ. There are many bad habits that we can fall into as church members. We can grow tired of regularly attending worship services or Bible study. Little by little, we can begin to slip away until we realize that there are more Sundays and Wednesdays when we are absent than when we actually attend. The Bible that we know we should read daily often sits idly on the bedside or the cabinet, just waiting until we remember what a helpful tool it can be.

Another bad habit is that of letting hurt feelings keep us away from regular attendance. There may have been some cause or event where we felt injured or slighted, and we begin to slip away from attending because of the injury that we received. We know about forgiveness, but it can be hard to practice when *we* are the ones who need to do the act of forgiving!

We can even begin to slip away from the love and joy we experience in Christ. It is true that God never stops loving us, but we sometimes distance ourselves from God's love. We become like Adam and Eve in the Garden of Eden when they turned away from God. God came looking for them, calling out, "Where are you?" Did God not know where they were? I believe that God did know, and that God knows where we are today. We cannot hide from God, but we do sometimes purposefully distance ourselves from God. When this happens, we only hurt ourselves. We miss out on the joy and peace that come from a relationship with Christ. There can be newness each day when we walk faithfully with him.

That is what renewal is all about: renewing our love for Jesus Christ and experiencing the freshness of a relationship that brings joy to our lives each day. When we find ourselves miles away from our Heavenly Father, we can experience the same redemption as the Prodigal Son, who came to his senses when eating with the pigs and determined to go home and beg his father to take him back. Our God is waiting at the end of the road for our return! You can experience joy, peace, security, and a love that never ends once again. And it starts with a simple step back to God. God doesn't ask you to beg or grovel; God just asks for you to come home.

A Time to Give Thanks

This is the season to give thanks. But quite frankly, sometimes we don't want to give thanks. When we have experienced a loss. When we have experienced turmoil at work. When we learn that a loved one has a debilitating or terminal disease. On those days, it is hard to say thanks with any sense of conviction. If you are there at this time, please know that you are not alone. God isn't scared of your anger, hurt, or pain. In fact, I truly believe God embraces that pain. God welcomes your hurts. That's what the crucifixion of Jesus Christ was: an outlet for God to take all our frustrations, cares, and pains. In place of all that pain, God gives us peace, fulfillment, and joy. I remember vividly the year that our seventeen-month-old son Jake died. Each anniversary, birthday, and holiday was worse than the one before. Each day was a painful reminder that something special was missing from our lives.

There is hope. Life does continue, but we have to choose to keep going. We can choose to close up shop and become lost in a maelstrom of sorrow or grief, or we can choose to live for Christ in spite of our circumstances.

Maybe you are just beginning your walk of faith, maybe you have been a person of faith for a long time, or maybe you are just on the outside looking in trying to determine if all this faith stuff is real. Regardless of where you are right now, I encourage you to offer up a little prayer to God today. It doesn't have to be long. It doesn't have to be wordy. Just pray with a humble and honest heart. Simply say, "God, thank you!"

Enter into his gates with thanksgiving, and into his courts with praise; be thankful unto him, and bless his name. (Psalm 100:4, KJV)

We may sometimes give up on God, but God never gives up on us! Turning your hearts to heaven allows God to demonstrate how real God is in our world today. Sure, there are skeptics. Sure, there are the mass

numbers of people who say that religion is just a "crutch for the weak."
To them, I say you are exactly right! God at times is a crutch holding me
up when I cannot hold myself, but God is also so much more, and yes, I
need God precisely because I am weak. I need God because without that
constant guiding hand, life doesn't make much sense. I need God because
without God's grace, the pain of losing a loved one is too unbearable. I need
God because I have much to be thankful for, and I choose to honor and
thank God because I need something or someone to be thankful *to*!

In this vein, I want to thank God for each of you. You continue to be
so encouraging and loving to my family and me. Please come worship with
us this Sunday as we continue our discussion of giving thanks in Psalm 105.
I encourage you to bring someone with you who hasn't been to our church
before. Better yet, try to find someone who has never been to church before.
Let us help others know why we are so thankful!

And Justice For All

This week we once again set aside a special day to commemorate the life of Martin Luther King, Jr., the most notable civil rights leader of the 1960s. His assassination on April 4, 1968, in Memphis reminded the world of the dangers of speaking out against the status quo. He worked for many things, but especially for equality and justice for all people. Our national holiday is a living tribute to the dreams that Martin Luther King, Jr., had for our land.

The inauguration of President Barak Hussein Obama, also taking place on Martin Luther King Day, highlighted how far our land has come. President Obama even used a Bible belonging to Martin Luther King, Jr. as he took the oath of office.

On a recent trip to South Africa, my wife and I were confronted with the harsh realities of racial tension and division. We visited townships where thousands of people lived virtually on top of each other in homes no bigger than our pool shed and often without running water or electricity. Violence is an ever-present reality for those living in these conditions. AIDS is rampant. Yet, in the midst of such dire circumstances, people are continuing to live the words of Jesus Christ as interpreted through the message of Martin Luther King, Jr. One such ministry is Living Hope. Living Hope grew out of a local church that took seriously the call to reach out to those in their community who were not receiving just treatment. It was started by John Thomas, pastor of Fish Hoek Baptist Church in 2000. Living Hope ministers daily to the needs of townships and local communities including Capricorn, Masiphumelele, Mountain View, Muizenberg, Ocean View, Overcome Heights, and Red Hill. One of Living Hope's ministries is an after-school program that provides meals to its children. It also operates a hospital that cares for many who are turned away from other medical care and teaches hydroponic farming to people in the townships so that they can provide both food and income for their families. Living Hope also works with people suffering from various addictions. For more information on Living Hope, see www.livinghope.co.za/.

This week, as we remember the dreams of Martin Luther King, Jr., may we each be challenged to make a difference in our world today. No government or land is perfect, but we have much to celebrate and be thankful for. I pray that we will continue to fight for justice for the unprotected, the widow, the orphan, the poor, and anyone else who cannot speak up for themselves. May we continue to work together in fulfilling the quest for equality for everyone regardless of race, color, creed, or other cause of separation or isolation.

Another Year Has Passed

Yes, that is right. Another year has come and gone. Last Sunday my family and I celebrated my forty-ninth birthday. My, oh my, where have all the years gone? It wasn't your traditional birthday party. We were away for a family overnight road trip. There was no cake, no invitations, and no gifts. Just a few cards and the treasure of spending time together. But what a wonderful birthday!

In our busy world, one of the most valuable commodities any of us have is time. In that moment we have the opportunity to choose, for a few precious seconds, what we want to do. For years it seems like the church was not aware of a family's need for time together. There was always more to do at the church, and when we got there we were always going in different directions. But there is something sacred about a family spending time together: at play, at rest, at home, out in the community, or at church.

I am so grateful for every moment of those forty-nine years. In that time I have experienced completion of several educational degrees, a relationship with a lovely wife, the challenges and blessings of raising children, the blessing of finding meaningful work, and many, many other things. And in all those years, nothing seems more valuable than the simple gift of time. It is a gift just to spend a few moments with those we love.

Maybe that is what is so promising about our relationship with Jesus Christ: when this hectic life is over, we can experience eternity with those we care about most. And with that expanse of time, we have plenty of moments to make a lot of new friends as well!

Thanks to everyone for the well wishes and cards on my birthday this year. My prayer for you is that you enjoy your birthday this year just as much as I enjoyed mine!

Grace and peace.

Whew

It is Tuesday night, February 19, at 11 p.m. Since I left First Baptist Church of Bristol on Sunday morning, I have been in a whirlwind. This morning I spoke at chapel at Carson-Newman, bringing the message "The Search for Answers," from Job 28, which is the third of four messages dealing with suffering in the book of Job. President O'Brien, Don Garner, Bill and Carolyn Blevins, and I are tag-teaming this series in the month of February. Tonight, I took Brack, my oldest son and soon-to-be divinity school student, to hear Dr. Walter Brueggemann, a world-renowned Old Testament scholar, who spoke as part of a lecture series at Central Baptist Church of Bearden, our home church. I anticipate being able to have lunch with Dr. Brueggemann tomorrow with a small group of friends. I may float to church on Wednesday evening on small clouds!

Dr. Brueggemann spoke tonight on reading the prophetic texts of the Old Testament as grief therapy. There is a recent movement among Old Testament scholars to read many poetic texts of the prophets as writings designed to help the nations of Israel and Judah cope with great losses and prepare for a new day in exile and beyond.

Brueggemann applies these ideas to the United States and connects them to the need for lament or grief therapy in our pulpits today. He points out that much has been lost, and we are often grieving these losses even without articulating what they are. For example, we have lost the "golden age" of many evangelical churches when we could announce a revival or Bible study and hundreds would show up.

Brueggemann also correlates the prophetic texts of the Old Testament as grief therapy to our national political climate. Many pundits and politicians love to excite large groups of people with nationalistic sentiments about the greatness of our nation and exclaim that "we live in the greatest nation on the earth." Brueggemann reminds us of the realities of a growing global economy and community. As the prophets remind the people of Israel of their ongoing realities, Brueggemann calls upon us as modern people of faith to be mindful of the realities of our current situation. We are no longer the world's leader in the areas of education, manufacturing, medicine, healthcare, or a host of other areas. The prophetic texts of the Old Testament remind us that God did not abandon God's people, and God will not abandon us when we fervently turn to God in times of need.

May God bless you throughout this day and week. Please be in prayer for your family, your church staff, and the people of your local community.

Cast Your Cares upon God

10

Cast all your anxiety on him, because he cares for you. (1 Peter 5:7, NIV)

After years of visiting hospital waiting rooms to be present for families of sick loved ones, it is always a new experience when I am the one sitting in that room, anxiously awaiting the outcome of a medical procedure or surgery. This week has been another chapter of waiting for the outcome of a family member's surgery.

We are so grateful that the surgery went well and that Kim is home resting and recuperating. It meant so much that friends and even a church member from a former pastorate came to visit with Kim before the surgery. Another family friend sat with us for about an hour while Kim was actually in surgery. The gifts of time and presence are meaningful during times of anxiety and crisis.

Kim and I would are grateful to each of you for your prayers and support. During times of personal crisis, I am reminded of how 1 Peter 5:7 becomes personally applicable once again. This verse encourages us to offer our cares before the Lord. God is able to handle our stress and fears. Most of us know this verse and the principle it contains, but it is easy to quote and hard to live.

God is truly able to sustain us through any crisis. We exhibit our faith in him through prayer and patient waiting. Time after time, God has helped Kim and me through each family crisis. There will be other issues we must face, but God promises to walk with us through each struggle if we commit ourselves to walking with God.

Cast your cares upon God . . .

Don't Be a Christian Couch Potato

I'll never forget 1995. It was the best of times; it was the worst of times. My family and I had just moved from Clarksville, Indiana, to Amherst, Ohio, a suburb on the west side of the Greater Cleveland area. The Indians were playing well, and the coming fall promised us a season to follow the Cleveland Browns firsthand for the first time in more than twenty years. At our house we don't say "the Browns"; we say "THE BROWWWNNNSSSS!" But as many of you know, 1995 was the darkest year for Cleveland Browns fans. Art Modell decided that he alone could chart the future of football in the city of Cleveland, so on the promise of millions from the city of Baltimore, Modell moved the Browns there, and they became the Ravens. I was devastated. I determined that if the Browns were no more, then football was no more. The outcome of that decision was dramatic. I stopped watching football altogether, and what I learned is that I had become quite a weekend couch potato. In the first season without the Browns in fall 1996, I lost more than thirty pounds. No longer did I sit idly before a box and eat nachos, popcorn, or cookies. I also found that my energy level dramatically increased. Losing the Browns ultimately was a salvific experience for me.

Many Christians today have become "Couch Potato Christians." This phenomenon is described by the author of 2 Thessalonians 3:1-18. In verses 6-15, Paul encourages the Christians at Thessalonica to be industrious.

Paul encourages these Christians to *avoid idleness*. "Keep away from every brother who is idle" (v. 6). The word "idleness" is translated from the Greek *ataktos*. This word is generally translated two ways: (1) undisciplined actions or (2) lazy individuals. "Lazy individuals" may be the meaning found in verse 6. Paul encourages these believers to be active; don't be lazy! In verses 7-9, he reminds the community of faith of the work ethic he exemplified in their midst. This text is reminiscent of 1 Thessalonians 2:8-9: "we worked night and day in order not to be a burden . . . ."

In verse 10, Paul gives a special admonition, "If a man will not work, he shall not eat." This verse has been used since its inception as a proof-text for the Protestant/Puritan work ethic. Another way of stating this is that good things will happen to those who work hard. As Christians, we are to be willing to work hard in the tasks God has placed before us. We often remember this verse when we see a homeless person who is panhandling or looking for food. If he wants to make money, we think, let him work!

But two warnings should accompany this text. The first warning is to avoid being judgmental. We have all heard the phrase, "God only helps those who help themselves." This is a dangerous phrase because it can lead to a theology of works. If I only work hard enough, then God will bless me. Or, to say it another way, if I don't have much, then God hasn't blessed me, and God must not have blessed me because I didn't work hard enough! A better phrase is probably, "God helps those who cannot help themselves."

As Christians, we are called to be disciples of Jesus Christ and avoid idleness.

The second warning is not to equate discipleship with being a workaholic. We are to be willing to work hard for the sake of Christ, but we must also know how to relax and enjoy life and our families. Too many ministers' homes today are disasters—not because of the kind of people found in the family but simply because everyone in the church and community often comes before the minister's family.

We ought to encourage those who do most of the work of the ministry, whether paid or unpaid, to take time for themselves and their families.

Hard work for hard work's sake is not equivalent to holiness!

> He always said he would retire
> When he had made a million clear,
> And so he toiled into the dusk
> From day to day, from year to year.
>
> At last he put his ledgers up
> And laid his stock reports aside—

But when he started out to live
He found he had ALREADY DIED! (Author unknown)

May each of us be willing to work hard for the cause of Jesus Christ, but may we also remember the necessary Sabbaths in our lives. Each of us needs time to rest!

In a second major emphasis, Paul encourages the Christians at Thessalonica to *stay focused on the task at hand* (vv. 11-15). Paul encourages the readers of this letter not to lose their focus.

In verse 11 he writes, "They are not busy; they are busybodies." The Christian church is not a place for spectator Christianity. We come and buy our tickets with our tithes and offerings but never make it past the bench or the stands within the church. We come and talk about the Christian life, but we rarely live it. We come and talk about reaching a lost and dying world for Christ, but we rarely share it. We come and talk about the hungry and the homeless, but we rarely feed them or give them shelter.

We know what to do, so let's get busy! Paul also encourages us never to tire in doing what is right (v. 13). Don't give up!

In verses 14 and 15, Paul encourages the church to ostracize those who are couch potatoes and unwilling to work, not because they're our enemies but because they're our friends and we should hold them accountable.

Paul ends this second letter to the Thessalonians by sealing it with the writing from his own hand (v. 17). The letter ends, as it begins, with the word "grace." God's grace is sufficient for the days of Paul, and it is sufficient for us today.

First and Second Thessalonians remind us of the parables Jesus used to teach his followers about his return. Many times his parables demonstrated to his followers that he would indeed leave them, but he promised to return.

Matthew 25 provides a trilogy of such parables. In Matthew 25:1-13, Jesus tells the story about the ten virgins who were waiting for the bridegroom to come. Matthew 25:14-30 describes the master who left and gave varying amounts of talents to his servants. In Matthew 25:31-46, Jesus uses a parable of the sheep and goats to describe the accountability of all people for our belief in Jesus Christ.

We all have twenty-four hours a day. Who is the master of your time?

Don't Let Me Drown in Shallow Water

Given as a devotion at the Carson-Newman Faculty meeting on September 15, 2011.

It is Passion Week, and Easter is on the other side. This was a week of uncertainty and trial for Jesus. It is reminiscent of the descriptions in Psalm 57:1-6: "until this violent storm has past . . . those who are out to get me . . . surrounded by fierce lions . . . whose tongues cut like swords . . . my enemies have set a trap for me . . . ."

I can't speak for you, but it sounds to me like the author of this psalm may be a professor of religion at a Baptist college or university! It is amazing to me how much external pressure is constantly exerted on faculty, administrators, and staff to worship at either of the polar idols: fundamentalism or liberalism. God help the person who simply wants to be Christ-like.

Why in the world would anyone willingly spend so much time earning degrees in higher education only to live daily in the boiling cauldron of religious political instability?

Like the author of Psalm 57, we often feel that we need an advocate or someone who can bring justice into an unjust environment. We look to heroes who serve as examples and inspirations to motivate us to continue our chosen journeys.

William Augustus Jones is one such hero. He was born on February 24, 1934, in Louisville, Kentucky, and he passed away on February 4, 2006. Dr. Jones was an African-American minister and civil rights leader. He attended the University of Kentucky, graduating with honors in sociology.

He regretted that he was not allowed to play basketball there because "persons of color" were then barred from the team. He earned a doctorate from the Crozer Theological Seminary.

In 1961 he joined the Reverend Martin Luther King, Jr. in splitting from the Conservative Baptist Convention and forming the Progressive National Baptist Convention. William Augustus Jones was never afraid to speak his mind. He often made controversial statements and led many controversial causes in the New York City area. At the height of his ministry, he led the Bethany Baptist Church in Brooklyn with its 5,000 members and hosted a syndicated radio program called the Bethany Hour. In 1979 he published his only book, *God in the Ghetto*.

Jones often told the story about how a young mother came to him and asked him to look after her baby boy. This baby boy became a Pentecostal minister when he was ten years old. Jones later enlisted this young person to become active in a ministry in his church to feed the poor—Operation Breadbasket. In 1994, this now well-known public figure came to Bethany Baptist Church and was re-baptized as a Baptist. You know him today as the Reverend Al Sharpton.

I had the pleasure of meeting William Augustus Jones at the annual Campbell University Ministers' Conference in Buies Creek, North Carolina. Jones had the voice of God! A deep, melodious tempo that made you take notice of every word uttered from his mouth. I will never forget Jones sharing with us the prayer that he said he prayed every day of his life.

Lord, let me have some mourners at my funeral, don't let my body outlast my mind, and keep me from drowning in shallow water.

As we reflect on the gravity of the work to which we are called, as we encounter those who want us to fail, let us remember the prayer of this wise minister: "Lord, keep me from drowning in shallow water."

Happy Easter.

13

Expecting the Unexpected

When I arrived at my office this morning, I was greeted by shards of ceiling tile lying all over my computer work station. A telephone table behind where my chair usually sits was covered with water and pieces of wet tile. Many notes and copies of lectures, tests, and sundry items were covered with debris and water. The corner of my office was a mess. There was obviously a leak between the second and third floors of my building and my office was catching the brunt of it. Fortunately, none of my vast collection of books was damaged by this incident.

Such things never seem to happen at an opportune time. I am fortunate that this mess occurred over the weekend without me being under the leak and that I caught it before the situation worsened. Nonetheless, it is still a mess. The corner where this happened housed many of my papers, files, and stacks of things that were out of sight and out of mind.

Life seems to happen this way for many of us. Illnesses, auto breakdowns, home catastrophes, or broken appliances all bombard us at the most inopportune times of life. These things happen to us all. So we pick up, clean up, and get started once again.

When talking with couples planning a wedding, I always remind them that Murphy's Law always seems present in and around the wedding ceremony. For those of you who need a refresher, Murphy's Law simply says, "Anything that can go wrong will go wrong." I always encourage these couples that whatever goes wrong can be dealt with if we keep our senses of flexibility and humor. At our wedding, Kim had a flat tire on the way to the church for the service. A family friend of mine happened to stop by and help her. When we arrived at the hotel on our honeymoon trip, Kim discovered that she had forgotten her shoes and her makeup for the trip. Murphy's Law was making itself known. Yes, the honeymoon was a little shorter because of it, but it was still a getaway that we will always remember.

In some ways, such interruptions are the real blessings of life. When faced with them, my father always said, "Don't panic!" Of course that admonition never lasted long, and he was usually the one who helped fan the overall cloud of panic, but the words of encouragement were still the right thing to say.

We often discover that these untimely interruptions are not mere accidents or coincidences but the opportunity to witness God in action in our lives and the world today. Many of us never question our lives until we are "interrupted." Time after time, the Bible gives witness to God's interruption into people's lives. Moses was tending sheep in a forgotten wasteland when he encountered God through a mysterious burning bush. Daniel was a political prisoner in a foreign land when God broke into his world through the unwanted attention of the land's king. The disciples who met Jesus certainly weren't looking for a new vocation when they were asked to follow him. Saul of Tarsus was traveling throughout the land, actually persecuting people who were followers of Jesus, when God used blindness to allow him to truly see!

It is hard to expect the unexpected. It can also be painful. Someone once commented that there is often a hallway between the door that has just closed before you and the door that is open, and that hallway is sometimes referred to as "hell." These unexpected interruptions in my life have sometimes been terribly difficult. But I am thankful that God has used these timely interruptions to provide for me the opportunities to grow and develop in my walk with God.

As for this disheveled office, I guess it was about time to finally clean up that corner!

Blessings on your week and all its interruptions.

Celebrating Our Core Values 1: Bible Freedom

This weekend, June 20–23, Baptists from around the world are gathering in Fort Worth, Texas, for this year's Cooperative Baptist Fellowship General Assembly. It is a time of worship. It is a time for celebration. It is a time for Christians to gather and reacquaint themselves with other like-minded followers of Jesus Christ.

Over the last twenty years, the Cooperative Baptist Fellowship has provided progressive Baptist churches the opportunity to work together toward common purposes and goals. In *The Baptist Identity: Four Fragile Freedoms* (Macon GA: Smyth & Helwys Publishers, 1993), Walter Shurden outlines four core values that Baptists celebrate—in other words, what makes one a Baptist. These are Bible Freedom, Soul Freedom, Church Freedom, and Religious Freedom.

The first core value is Bible Freedom. Shurden writes, "Bible Freedom is the historic Baptist affirmation that the Bible, under the Lordship of Christ, must be central in the life of the individual and church and that Christians, with the best and most scholarly tools of inquiry, are both free and obligated to study and obey the scripture" (9). Simply put, we who claim to be Baptist are people of the Book!

The Bible has always had a central place in my home. As a youngster I remember being given my first Bible by my parents. At age five or six, I actually found one of the passages during a church Bible drill and read the Scripture in front of all the adults. My parents decided then and there that if I could find a Scripture reference before a room full of adults, then it was time for me to have my own Bible.

Later in Vacation Bible School, I won a fishing pole because I memorized more Bible verses than all the other young people in my age group. It didn't hurt to include short passages of Scripture like Psalm 117, the shortest psalm, or John 11:35, "Jesus wept."

Driving three hours to attend Oklahoma Baptist University, I picked up a hitchhiker along the interstate before my first semester away at college. After a long conversation about faith and the Bible, I gave my personal Bible to the hitchhiker. It didn't occur to me that I had Old and New Testament that semester, and I had just given away a textbook that I would need. Seven of my new friends learned from my roommate what I had done, and before the class started, these great young people pooled their money and purchased a New International Version Bible for me. I still have that Bible, and it sits proudly on my desk at my home all the time. I use it devotionally every day, and it is on its third binding! God's word has always been an important part of my life.

Many people know a lot of things about the Bible. Too many people, however, know things about the Bible but have actually never read many parts of it. Your canon, or your body of Scripture, is really only what you have actually read of the Bible. If there are parts of the Bible you have not read, then how can you claim that the Bible is in fact your guide for living? The Bible is alive and active, but only when you and I activate it by reading it and giving it life through how we live. We must also recognize that the Living Word is also known as Jesus Christ. As we seek to be people of the Book, we are aiming to be followers of the Living Word, Jesus Christ.

I encourage you to be a person of the Book. Take time this coming year to develop the discipline to read through the entirety of God's word. The Bible is clearly a special book, a sacred book, but it makes a difference in our lives only when we take time to read its pages and apply them to our day-to-day activities!

15

Celebrating Our Core Values 2: Soul Freedom

Please accept a heartfelt thank-you from Kim, Zachary, and me for the warm reception dinner you put together last week. We enjoyed the fellowship, the food, and the fun immensely. We are humbled by your gracious reception, and we are thankful to be with you during this time of hope and anticipation.

Last week I began to look at the first of the four fragile freedoms enjoyed by Baptist believers as set forth by Walter Shurden in his work, *The Baptist Identity* (Macon GA: Smyth & Helwys Publishing, 1993). This week I would like to introduce you to the second of these freedoms: soul freedom. Shurden defines soul freedom as "the historic Baptist affirmation of the inalienable right and responsibility of every person to deal with God without the imposition of creed, the interference of clergy, or the intervention of the civil government" (23).

Many other terms are often used to describe this basic belief. It is sometimes called "soul liberty," "the competency of the soul before God," or "the priesthood of the believer." In recent years this basic core belief has been under constant attack by some who wish to mandate their own set of rules and regulations over other individual Christians, churches, associations, and state institutions. Sometimes, one church tries to administer pressure on another church to conform to their way of thinking on a doctrinal or spiritual issue or practice. It can happen also inside the body of a church when one person or group tries to coerce a congregation to follow their "approved" type of religious conviction.

Soul freedom calls us to individual responsibility before God. You and you alone are responsible for your relationship to God and the belief system by which you live. As a body of believers in a church, we come together cooperatively to do the work of ministry and to pool our resources. Baptists, however, are not to be subject to the "thought police" who try to manipulate our behavior to some prescribed ideal. Churches operate with a constitution and bylaws that help to govern or guide our working relationships, but these rules apply to our working together as an organization—not to our salvation or to test our faith before God. Baptists for the most part have been a confessional people, not a creedal people. We serve side by side with each other. We worship side by side with each other. We work together to bring about the common good for the kingdom of God. In doing this, we still maintain our individual freedoms and beliefs.

Some churches also have a church covenant. For many of them, this is a document that came from some outside agency and was adopted by the church at an early stage in its history. If we went line by line through each issue in the covenant, we might find an item with which we either disagree or do not practice. The beauty of soul freedom is that no one in the church should be watching over your shoulder to actively enforce each and every line of any document, including a covenant. While these items represent a large body of beliefs for which most agree, and many wholeheartedly, soul freedom says that I am free under the Lordship of Jesus Christ, and so are you.

The late Herschel Hobbs, a famous Baptist layman and statesperson, wrote, "So in reality Baptists are the most broad-minded of all people in religion. They grant to every man the right that he shall be free to believe as he wants. But they insist upon the same right for themselves. The moment that a Baptist seeks to coerce another person—even another Baptist—in matters of religion, he violates the basic belief of Baptists" (*The Baptist Faith and Message*, 1971, p. 10)

The "competency of the Soul" was a hallmark of E. Y. Mullins, who wrote about this concept in his book at the turn of the twentieth century titled *The Axioms of Religion* (repr., Macon GA: Mercer University Press, 2010). Mullins championed that in matters of faith and practice, people are free to choose but remain responsible for our choices. Mullins noted that we are ultimately responsible only to God, not to other people. It is little wonder that those who seek to manipulate and control others in matters of faith and practice have strived to diminish the contributions and character of early Baptist leaders like Mullins.

The term "Baptist" does not have to be a byword or a word that makes us feel ashamed. We have a rich and diverse heritage. Soul freedom reminds us that we choose how we worship and live before a living and Holy God. Soul freedom also reminds us that we have a choice where we worship God. I pray that you will continue to practice your soul freedom as an active participant at the First Baptist Church of Bristol: a place where you can find freedom, forgiveness, and the love of Jesus Christ alive and well!

16

Celebrating Our Core Values 3: Church Freedom

Happy Independence Day! At a time when we as a nation celebrate our freedom, let us take a moment to celebrate our freedom as a body of believers. The third freedom mentioned by Walter "Buddy" Shurden in his book *The Baptist Identity: Four Fragile Freedoms* is church freedom. He defines church freedom as "the historic Baptist affirmation that local churches are free, under the Lordship of Christ, to determine their membership and leadership, to order their worship and to work, to ordain whom they perceive as gifted for ministry, male or female, and to participate in the larger Body of Christ, of whose unity and mission Baptists are proudly a part" (33).

Penrose St. Amant, a church historian from Louisiana, gave his life to theological education by serving as a professor of Church History at New Orleans Baptist Theological Seminary and The Southern Baptist Theological Seminary, and as president at the International Baptist Theological Seminary in Ruschlikon, Switzerland. Kim and I were neighbors to Penrose St. Amant and his wife for one year at Golden Gate Baptist Theological Seminary. This couple gave a year of their retirement to teach at Golden Gate. They would walk their little dog, "Swiss Boy," every day. My first encounter with this family came when I was walking from my truck to my apartment. "Swiss Boy" ran around a corner and latched onto my new ostrich skin cowboy boots that I had received as a gift. About the time I was ready to launch this nuisance that had attached itself to my ankle, the St. Amants arrived to rescue their beloved pet. My plans for launching this "ankle biter" quickly turned into introductions to my new friends. (On a side note, "Swiss Boy" died at Golden Gate when the St. Amants were out walking him. He encountered a much larger dog that scared him, and he died from apparent heart failure. The owner paid for a trip to Europe so "Swiss Boy II" could be procured. The dog was simply that beloved.)

Penrose St. Amant described the church in these terms: "a community of folk for whom Jesus Christ was Savior and Lord" ("Our Baptist Heritage and the Church," *Baptist History and Heritage* 2/2 [July 1967]: 88). This is a simple yet powerful definition of what it means to be a church. We are a gathering of people under the Lordship of Jesus Christ. In some church traditions, one person is responsible for all the official decisions of the church. This is true of the Roman Catholic tradition, with the final say resting on the Pope, and it is equally true of some independent-minded churches where a single figure, usually a pastor, is empowered to make all the crucial decisions. In some traditions, a small number of individuals or clergy make the important decisions together concerning the work of the church. But as Shurden states in writing about church freedom, Baptists are in theory working under a "Christocracy" (37) where the people are all under the Lordship of Jesus Christ equally. Shurden explains that pragmatically, this is worked out in a democratic style of governance where the vote of the people is entrusted to bring about the will of Christ in the church. This can sometimes be messy. It can sometimes be cumbersome and slow. But it is the Baptists' way. Every member of a Baptist church should have equal say and equal vote in deciding the working of the church. In theological terms, this is known as the congregational model of leadership.

I thank God that I live in a free country and belong to a free church. Let us celebrate our freedom and use it to go about the mission of the church: to reach others with the good news of Jesus Christ, to care for the needs of the sick and dying in our community, to stand with the oppressed and those who are seeking justice and equality, to worship regularly with our fellow believers in the name of Jesus Christ, and to continue to be a reminder to a world that a loving and compassionate God has not abandoned them. Let freedom ring!

Celebrate your independence!

17

Celebrating Our Core Values 4: Religious Freedom

The fourth and final freedom discussed by Walter Shurden in his work *The Baptist Identity: Four Fragile Freedoms* is religious freedom. Shurden defines it as "the historic Baptist affirmation of freedom OF religion, freedom FOR religion, and freedom FROM religion, insisting that Caesar is not Christ and Christ is not Caesar" (45).

This freedom has become increasingly problematic in many Baptist churches in America today. It is easier for us who are Baptists to champion religious freedom when we are in a weak or powerless position. For many centuries, Baptists have found themselves as the minority among religious and civic entities. In these times, voices of great Baptist leaders like Thomas Helwys sounded a clarion call for freedom of religion. Helwys wrote in 1612, "mens religion to God is betwixt God and themselves" (*A Short Declaration of the Mistery of Iniquity* as cited in William Estep, *Revolution Within the Revolution: The First Amendment in Historical Context, 1612–1789* [Grand Rapids MI: Eerdmans Publishing Company, 1990]). We remember from the pages of our United States history that many (but not all) of the waves of immigrants who first colonized our great land were seeking religious freedom. Many simply wanted to live in a place where they could be peaceable and practice their own system of religious beliefs without fear of reprisals or punishment by the state or persecution by other religious groups.

In 2012, Baptists have become a powerful political, economic, and cultural force in the United States of America, especially in the Southeast. In the past twenty years, even many Baptists have begun to question the historic principle of religious freedom. One prominent Baptist pastor, who at the time led the largest congregation within the Southern Baptist Convention, said during a television interview in 1984, "I believe this notion of separation of church and state was the figment of some infidel's imagination" (quoted in Shurden, 51–52). How easy it is for us to take our freedom for granted in times of prosperity.

Do we really believe in religious freedom today? Is this freedom worth fighting for in our society? I believe, alongside Shurden, that it is vital for the health of our world that Baptists take up this mantle once again. It is easy for us to support the concept of religious freedom when we consider the lack of freedom many believers have had in places like the former Communist country of Russia. I taught at the St. Petersburg Evangelical Theological Academy in 2004, 2007, and 2010 in St. Petersburg, Russia. In my travels there, I was amazed at the transformation of this once Communist country where churches were turned into state buildings. Now, Christians are experiencing the opportunity to express religious freedom however they choose. But in the midst of this transformation, another danger lies in the background. The Russian Orthodox Church has often seriously curtailed efforts of Protestant churches in outreach and growth. Though the Communists no longer control the government, this control has been replaced by the power of a "state" church where all other forms of religious expression must be approved, either formally or informally, by the Russian Orthodox Church.

We, who are Baptists in the South, are in danger of being more like the former Communists of Russia, or the now powerful Russian Orthodox Church, in matters of religious practice. If we truly believe in religious freedom, are we willing to extend freedom to Christians who do not practice their faith as we do, or to non-Christian religions? Are we willing to extend that freedom to those who profess no religious beliefs? Here in Tennessee, many in the city of Murfreesboro have been battling over the building of a new mosque. Local Baptists have led the opposition to this development. At the current time, a battle is being waged over the right of those of Muslim faith to occupy this new construction. Are we to support the First Amendment of the United States Constitution, which says, *Congress shall make no law respecting an establishment of religion, or prohibiting the free exercise thereof?*

I believe the answer to that question is a resounding YES! I may not agree with the beliefs of others, and I may lament the lack of belief of so many people in our world, but I believe that religious freedom calls me to respect and support the individual religious rights of all.

Praise God for our religious freedom.

Historic Bristol VA/TN slogan sign, which spans State Street near the Train Station.
Photo by Ben J. Butler

Bristol Public Library, jointly owned by Bristol, TN, and Bristol, VA.
Photo by Ben J. Butler

Bristol, VA, Post Office located in Bristol,TN.
One end is Bristol, VA, and the other is Bristol, TN.
Photo by Ben J. Butler

Entrance to Blakley-Mitchell Business, a landmark in downtown Bristol
Photo by Ben J. Butler

Cameo Theatre with loft apartments in buildings on either side.
Photo by Ben J. Butler

Plaque on the transportation building at the Farmers' Market
Photo by Ben J. Butler

Site of the hotel where the Bristol recordings were made in 1927.

Photo by Ben J. Butler

Country Music Mural and Stage at the Farmers' Market

Photo by Ben J. Butler

Walking
the Street

Prayer Changes Things

18

James writes, "Is any one of you in trouble? He should pray. Is anyone happy? Let him sing songs of praise. Is anyone sick? He should call the elders of the church to pray over him and anoint him with oil in the name of the Lord. And the prayer offered in faith will make the sick person well; the Lord will raise him up. If he has sinned, he will be forgiven. Therefore confess your sins to each other and pray for each other so that you may be healed. The prayer of a righteous man is powerful and effective." (James 5:13-16)

Anecdotes seem trite sometimes in regard to the power of prayer. But since I just returned from Oklahoma and was able to spend my father's sixty-eighth birthday with him, let me share of the power of prayer in the life of my father and my family.

In the early 1970s, my father worked at the Port of Muskogee for Williams Pipeline Corporation, loading and unloading barges that had come up the Arkansas River. He oversaw the process of loading several tons of steel pipes and metal on long trailers that were then shipped all over the Southwest. These barges often came from other continents to be unloaded in Muskogee, Oklahoma. One day when I got off the school bus, I was greeted by a neighbor who informed me that my father had been in an accident, and I needed to stay at her house until my mother could come and get me.

It was quite an accident! A whole load of steel had slipped off a truck, knocked my father to the ground, and rested on his feet. Every bone in one foot and ankle were broken. His other ankle and several bones in that foot were also broken. The original prognosis was not promising. The doctors tried to be optimistic, but they honestly projected that my father would never walk again. Our little church, the Keefeton Trinity Baptist Church, began to pray. Within six months, my father was walking with the help of various aids. At the end of the first year, he was walking on his own accord. By the eighteen-month mark, my father was back playing church softball—as the pitcher! And though he could never play shortstop or centerfield again, he was playing and doing what the doctors never thought possible.

There is amazing power when God's people come together and pray. Yes, the change of weather is a real pain for my father, and I can forget about getting through airport security in a timely fashion with him. Both ankles were surgically reconstructed, and there are too many pins in his feet to count. But my dad can walk, and he can almost run. Prayer changes things.

I am naïve enough to believe that God is looking down at us and waiting to use each of us when we turn to him. Yes, each of you has unique talents that may be used for the kingdom of God. Yes, we can make a commotion by our own power and might. But this church can only be set on fire by the indwelling of God's Holy Spirit. This comes when God's people begin to take God's word seriously and bathe each and every task that we attempt in prayer. It is the fuel that energizes the engine of God.

Most important, prayer changes *me*! It reminds me that I am nothing without the indwelling of God's Holy Spirit. It challenges me to be willing to change when my heart grows cold and I leave the path that Christ has set before me. It is the vehicle that enables me to have a proper relationship with Jesus Christ.

Yes, call me naïve, but I believe that prayer changes things.

19

What We Say Can Hurt

We have all heard the expression, "Sticks and stones may break my bones, but words will never harm me." The truth, though, is that words can hurt. They can drive people away, sometimes permanently. The issue of the place of words in our world is witnessed in many places throughout Scripture.

Proverbs 11:9 says, "Evil words destroy one's friends; wise discernment rescues the godly" (NLT). It appears (like many of the aphorisms found in the book of Proverbs) that this expression circulated in the ancient Near East as a wisdom saying, much like the modern proverbs of today, such as "A stitch in time saves nine," or "A bird in the hand is worth two in the bush."

Have you noticed the effects of negative speech? There are some people we don't want to be around because everything they say seems negative. The positive response to the negative phrase in the first part of Proverbs 11:9 is that good words bring welcomed results.

Proverbs 25:11 adds, "Timely advice is as lovely as golden apples in a silver basket" (NLT). This proverb places the work of speech in a better light. Kind or thoughtful words can provide healing in a troubled world. Careful speech brings light amid darkness.

We sometimes find ourselves like the apostle Peter, never truly stopping to think about the efficacy or power of our speech. Matthew 26:31-35 recounts Peter speaking brashly. He says that even if everyone else turns away from Jesus, he will surely not desert his friend. But not long after, he denied knowing Jesus three times. Let us carefully consider our words.

I have a good friend who always takes a long time when preparing to speak even in casual conversations. Mutual friends describe him as "the man who is constantly searching for a verb." It often takes him twice as long as someone else to tell a story or contribute to the conversation. But at least he truly has something to say when he speaks. Is it not better to consider our words carefully rather than having to apologize later for saying something we did not intend?

It is not a coincidence that the wisdom writings of the New Testament include a major section on the careful use of speech. The form of James's writing takes such a practical approach that many early Christians wondered about its usefulness in the Christian canon. Martin Luther even called James "a right strawy epistle."

James has always been one of my favorite books of the New Testament. It is earthy and real. It calls us to take action on the hypothetical elements of our faith.

In James 3:1-12, James says many things about the tongue and speech. In verses 9-12, he says that we should be consistent with our speech. While living in a world where people are carefully watching to see if what we profess is real and relevant, our speech and actions become vitally important.

What are some ways that we can use our gift of speech in a positive manner for Christ this week? Are there places in your life where you must adjust your speech to coincide with what you claim as a Christian?

Sticks and stones can break my bones, but words can and will really hurt me! And they hurt others too.

20

Lessons

As for me, God forbid that I should boast about anything except the cross of our Lord Jesus Christ. Because of that cross, my interest in this world died long ago, and the world's interest in me is also long dead. It doesn't make any difference now whether we have been circumcised or not. What counts is whether we really have been changed into new and different people. May God's mercy and peace be upon all those who live by this principle. They are the new people of God. (Galatians 6:14-16, NLT)

For the many of you who were able to be at church on Sunday, you know that we have started a new series on Sunday morning titled "Lessons." Our first lesson was "Lessons from the Slopes," and we investigated the commonality between the Christian walk and snow skiing. Next Sunday, the second message of the series is "Lessons from the Farm." The third installment will be "Lessons from the Rail Yard," followed by "Lessons from the Gym, or Nordic Track Christianity."

I wanted to say thanks to each of you for allowing me the freedom to try something creative in the preaching ministry here at First Baptist Church. I also wanted to clarify that even though the sermons are called "Lessons," I certainly do not have the Christian walk or God all figured out. These lessons grow out of the observations that I have made through walking the Christian journey and seeing it through various lenses and in various ways. Most sermons are not born out of deep theological reading or intentionally writing a sermon, even though some do grow out of this type of study. Most of the ideas that I have had over the years, however, have grown out of the back of riding a tractor, pushing a lawn mower, or spending time with a hoe tending to a garden. It seems that in the everyday things of life, God is there speaking to us along the way. Often it requires us to take our thoughts off of our individual situations and cares long enough for God to break in and speak to us.

As Paul relates above, I hope these sermons are not viewed as "boasting" or simply taken as entertainment. I pray that they can be helpful for others who are walking the Christian faith and looking for encouragement. Paul states, "What counts is whether we have been changed into new and different people." I hope that you have experienced the transforming power of Jesus Christ in your life so that when people see you, they actually see the person and presence of Jesus. Without that personal transformation, these lessons don't make much difference. They become quaint teaching, but not the essential fountain of nourishment that God's word can bring.

Another purpose for this series is to simply remind us that the Christian life has practical application. If we are not careful, we can become so "heavenly minded" that we lose our ability to have an earthly effect on those around us. We are not just a missions-minded church. We are a body of believers who are actively involved in supporting, praying for, and participating in the work of Jesus Christ in all that we do.

21

Let It Go Already

I just got back from my favorite lunch spot, El Sazon, located on Broadway in Jefferson City. God has a way of working on us even while we are on break at lunch. During my lunch break, a person with whom I've had a contentious relationship over the past couple of years walked into the restaurant. Immediately, all my feelings of contention and frustration surfaced once again. Then, wham, a certain post appeared on my Facebook page as I ate an order of chicken wings. A friend from North Carolina who was a member of a church I served in as an interim pastor wrote, "When we are angry or bitter it spills over on others. But so does happiness! Smile! God loves you!"

Really, God? Am I not entitled to even a little bit of selfishness and a childish attitude?

You already know the answer. No. I'm not entitled to that. When we hold bitterness or grudges in our hearts, we only hurt ourselves. Most of the time, the party that offended us, or that we feel offended us, doesn't even notice or remember the infraction in question. We need to let it go already!

But come on, Wayne, you say. Surely you are better than that! On most days I would like to think so, but then that person walks into the room, and my feelings of frustration, hurt, and bitterness surface. Without God's help, none of us can forgive and move beyond feelings like those. But with God's help, we can forgive, forget, and move on to celebrate the joys of life that God sets before us.

In a church the size of the First Baptist of Bristol, there may be someone (or some ones) who have offended you over the course of your time here. Chances are that they aren't even aware of their offense. I encourage you— no, I beg you—to let go of the hurt, bitterness, and anger that can so easily swell up inside of us. Forgive them already. Love them already. In doing so, you release your heart to heal and to begin to soar with the wings of the Spirit.

I will never forget a man who was a member of my first full-time pastorate in Amherst, Ohio. He was an elderly gentleman who lived with his elderly wife and pestered her to death. I went to see them on a regular basis. In fact, I made more trips to see them than to any other families in that church. He loved to share with me how active he had been in a church more than fifty years ago, and how if I just listened to him our church would be transformed. He relished sharing what a lousy job I had done as a pastor. His wife came to church regularly, but he could never seem to find the time to make it. One day I received a phone call from his wife, who informed me that they were going to leave the church because we weren't meeting their needs. She and her husband had been watching a televangelist, and they had decided to join that "tele-church." I assured her of my love and support and wished them both the best success. The next night, the gentleman had a massive stroke. The first person the wife called was not the pastor of that "tele-church"; it was yours truly.

In some ways, that was a tough hospital visit. In other ways, it was another opportunity to help a family in need. The elderly gentleman survived, and he lived for about three weeks after I left that church.

Matthew 6:14-15 says, "If you forgive those who sin against you, your heavenly Father will forgive you. But if you refuse to forgive others, your Father will not forgive your sins" (NLT).

Let it go already.

Love Is in the Air

"Entreat me not to leave you
Or to return from following you;
For where you go I will go,
And where you lodge I will lodge,
Your people will be my people
And your God my God." (Ruth 1:16, RSV)

This is the summer of weddings for me. On June 15, 2013, my oldest son, Brack, will wed Courtney Nicole Lockamy at Shiloh Baptist Church in Garner, North Carolina. Our families are both excited about this union and the opportunities for our children to grow into their own family unit.

In addition to our family wedding, I am honored to be asked to officiate several others this summer. Each union has required at least four to five hours of additional counseling along with the logistical preparation for the wedding event itself. Someone recently asked me how many weddings I have performed over the years. The real truth is that I have no idea how many I have done in thirty years of ministry.

Some weddings I have done were large, grand affairs complete with video cameras located throughout the ceremony and reception for posterity or for others who watched from a distance. Other weddings were small, quiet events with only the bride and groom present and my wife and me as the only witnesses. But regardless of the size of the celebration, the union is the same. It is the giving of oneself to join with another person in marriage.

The passage from Ruth 1:16 is often used as the basis for vows exchanged between husbands and wives. The original context for this passage was Ruth's proclamation to her mother-in-law, Naomi. Regardless of the earlier context, the meaning is clear: "I am committed to you!"

Kim and I look forward to celebrating twenty-eight years together as husband and wife. There is no magic formula we have found for success in marriage. But the vows in Ruth are a great place to start for marital bliss. "I am committed to you!"

For those of you who are married, how strong is your commitment to your spouse? Did you vow to love that person till death parts you? Kim often comments that she never considers divorce, but she does consider murder from time to time. This humor shows that we are committed to one another. Let me encourage you to make your commitment to your spouse a picture of your commitment to Christ.

"I am committed to you!"

Our Excuses Don't Matter to God

At a baseball sports banquet several years ago, a teacher and former coach from Southern Kentucky came and spoke to Brack's team. He is now a teacher at Central High School in Knoxville, Tennessee.

He told the group how he came from a poor family with little to no opportunities for bettering himself. The year he graduated from high school, Kentucky was rated dead last in education among the fifty states. The county he lived in was also last of all the counties in the common-wealth of Kentucky. There were two high schools, and his school was in second place educationally out of the two. When he graduated and the class ranking came out, he was deemed to be dead last in his graduating class. He kindly refers to himself as the Worst High School Graduate in America in the year he graduated.

In spite of all this, he continues to challenge young people through his life today. He encourages them to overcome obstacles and not to accept excuses. He has been successful in spite of limited opportunities, and we, too, can be successful if we are willing to work hard enough, not quit, and put our faith in a kind and loving God.

In Judges 6 we learn of another person who had limited opportunities. God came to Gideon and called him to lead his people in armed resistance against the Midianites. When God approached Gideon, he was beating out the wheat in hiding so the Midianites would not find him or the grain! The angel of the Lord said, "The LORD is with you, you mighty warrior" (v. 12). Gideon explained that he was *not* a mighty warrior and that the angel had the wrong man! The angel challenged Gideon to follow God's call to lead his people. Gideon responded, ". . . how can I deliver Israel? My clan is the weakest in Manasseh, and I am the least in my family" (v. 15).

As you read Judges 6–8, you learn how God does indeed use Gideon in a mighty way to deliver the people from the Midianites. There are many lessons in these pages, but I want to offer one for you to consider. God didn't accept any excuse from Gideon. God said, "Here's my plan. And you're the man, so let's get to it!"

What has God called us to do? What excuses have we offered to God? Let's stop resisting, trust God, and get to it!

May God's love challenge you to do acts of service in God's name.

Reaching Out

Whew, what a whirlwind this past week! Vacation Bible School, Sunday worship services, church-wide carnival, church-wide dinner, and Christian concert have made this last week busy for everyone. Several guests visited at one time or another during this stretch of frenetic activities.

Matthew 28:19-20 records what we now refer to as the Great Commission, the call to reach out to a world that needs to experience the love of Jesus Christ. The manner in which we share Christ's love is important. For many, evangelism is nothing more than trying to get a person to say the "sinner's prayer" and then rushing off to the next one. Some Christians on the other end of the spectrum never share their faith with others. For some it may be due to fear, insecurity, or a host of other reasons. We are not all called to be preachers or evangelists, but we can all share the love of Jesus Christ with others.

A contemporary word used in our churches today is "outreach." We, the First Baptist Church of Bristol, need to be intentional in reaching out to our friends and neighbors. Can you remember the last time you invited someone to Bible study on Sunday morning or encouraged someone to come to a worship service? A few people are open to attending a Bible study or service, but many are not. For them, it takes a one-on-one meeting outside the walls of a church building, or an invitation to an activity the church offers. In the next couple of weeks, we are hosting events designed to reach out to the people of our community and invite them to experience something inside the church apart from the typical Bible study or worship service.

All of us can reach out in our own way. You have the opportunity to reach people with the message of the gospel whom I could never reach.

Likewise, all of us can share our personal experience of living the Christian life. Your story and testimony matter to others, and they matter to God.

I have had the privilege of traveling to Israel on multiple occasions. Of all the places that I love to visit, the Dead Sea is a special treat. People enjoy swimming in the Dead Sea or caking themselves with the mud from its shores and bottom. Minimal wildlife is able to survive in the Dead Sea. There are no fish or regular creatures that we associate with our local lakes. If you want the experience of swimming in the Dead Sea, you can imitate it by filling your tub with mineral or baby oil. That's the way the water feels. It is a heavy, almost syrupy consistency. No one sinks in the Dead Sea due to the viscosity of the water.

Why is this body of water known as the Dead Sea? Quite simply, it is called the Dead Sea because it does not support life on its banks. There is no outlet for the water to escape. The Jordan River feeds the Dead Sea, but the water has nowhere to go. To parallel our earlier discussion, there is no reaching beyond itself. When we choose not to reach out, we are in essence choosing to stop growing and eventually to die. I pray that we will reach out together to everyone we meet throughout our day-to-day lives.

25

The Art of Fishing: Casting and Waiting

I have enjoyed fishing at various points in my life, but I do not consider myself a fisherman. When my parents moved to Oklahoma from Ohio, they settled in a little community called Elm Grove. It was nestled on the banks of Spaniard Creek, a tributary to the Arkansas River. Living near the creek was fortuitous for a youngster who loved the stories of Tom Sawyer and Huckleberry Finn. There were daily opportunities for bridge jumping, swimming, frog gigging, frog chasing, and of course fishing.

One weekend my father was out with a friend running trot and bottle lines on the Arkansas River. They returned in the morning after being out all night and brought home 150 pounds of catfish. During the day, Jimmy, the young son of my Dad's friend, and I went fishing for Sand Bass off the banks of the creek. We hit a hot streak where the fish were hitting literally everything we threw at them. We even tied two flies on the end of our line about 18 inches apart and caught them two at a time! It was the best fishing experience I have ever had.

Most of my fishing experiences include sitting and waiting for a single bite. There have been many more days when I didn't catch a single thing! Cast and wait, cast and wait, cast and wait. On those days, it is hard to be excited about the sport of fishing.

Reaching out to unbelievers can be a lot like fishing. Most days it is pretty difficult. Cast and wait, cast and wait, cast and wait. But then there are seasons when God's Spirit moves in an unbelievable way, and people start giving themselves to the movement of the Spirit and to following

Christ's personal call. These times make outreach an exciting experience. You never know what you will find until you start reaching out.

Sometimes it can be the greatest experience ever. Sometimes it can be sheer drudgery. But I have noticed one thing about true fishermen and fisherwomen: they never stop trying!

We are all called to be fishers of people. We are not responsible for the results. The results are left to the work of God's Spirit. We are, however, responsible for the effort.

"Come, follow me," Jesus said, "and I will make you fishers of men." At once they left their nets and followed him. (Matthew 4:19-20, NIV)

Let's go fishing!

26

The Joy of Giving

In all this I have given you an example that by such work we must support the weak, remembering the words of the Lord Jesus, for he himself said, "It is more blessed to give than to receive." (Acts 20:35, NRSV)

And I have been a constant example of how you can help the poor by working hard. You should remember the words of the Lord Jesus: "It is more blessed to give than to receive." (Acts 20:35, NLT)

I like to use this verse with my students around the time I give them the final exam in a course. In this instance, it is always better to give the exam than to receive the exam. But of course it also implies that the giver spent time making the exam, and ultimately must also spend time afterward grading it, so this may not be the best exegesis of the passage.

These words that Paul attributes to Jesus are not found in any of the Gospels. Similar words appear in early Christian writings such as I Clement and the *Didache*, but they are not found in Matthew, Mark, Luke, or John. Jesus says something similar in Luke 6:38: "If you give, you will receive. Your gift will return to you in full measure, pressed down, shaken together to make room for more, and running over. Whatever measure you use in giving—large or small—it will be used to measure what is given back to you" (NLT).

Each of these passages speaks of the joy of giving, even though the word "joy" is not actually used in any them. Joy comes when we know we have done the right thing, even when it requires self-sacrifice. I have never had many possessions or income to distribute to others, but I have had some great experiences in giving. When I graduated from high school,

I gave my best friend who was bound to a wheelchair my entire baseball and football trading card collection. It was a ragtag group of cards from the late 1950s through the late 1970s, including cards of Nolan Ryan, Reggie Jackson, Mickey Mantle, Brooks Robinson, and more. There were so many cards in this collection that he was able to start a trading card business, and his parents built him a shop and office next to his home. For the next decade, he ran that business with those cards as the foundation for getting started. There is joy in giving!

White Oak Missionary Baptist Church is a quiet, small congregation in the sand hills of Bladen County, North Carolina. I had the privilege of serving there as an interim pastor while teaching full-time at Campbell University. The church was filled with the usual members, gracious people who were blessings to visit with each week. I still maintain durable friendships with many from this congregation, including one man whom I had the pleasure of baptizing and with whom I meet to play our annual fall round of golf. In this church was a struggling single mother of several children. Her husband was not around, and she was in dire financial need. I brought this situation to my classes at Campbell, and out of five classes we raised more than $1,000 to give to this family just before Christmas. I had a cashier's check made to the mother, and we gave her the gift anonymously. Just last year, almost a decade later, I received a letter from one of her daughters, who was a senior religion major at Campbell University. She had received the Henderson Jake Ballard Scholarship and was writing to thank our family for creating the scholarship when our son Jake died in 2000. There is joy in giving!

You never know what God will do with your gift. But from my limited view, I can truly say that there is great joy in giving. This week we are celebrating an opportunity to pledge what we can give to the ministries of the First Baptist Church of Bristol. Please commit with me to pray about what we can give during the upcoming church year. Many of you are aware that the church's budget will be based on the amount of pledges that are received.

Let me encourage you to keep giving, as you are able, to charitable needs that are around you in everyday life. There are many worthy causes and people who are counting on you. But let me also encourage you to build a foundation of giving by committing your tithes and offerings to the ongoing work and ministry of this church. Together we can accomplish so much more than anything we can do individually.

There is joy in giving!

27

Vacation Bible School

Wow, this year is flying by! It is almost time for Vacation Bible School. VBS has become an annual event in most Baptist churches. It is a great time for children to come and celebrate being young people. There are friends, caring adults, games, prizes, cookies, Kool-Aid, and a host of fun things to do.

Vacation Bible School has been important to me. I can still remember a VBS when I was about twelve years old. Our pastor presented a gospel message to us ornery boys using Peanuts and Charlie Brown. I can still sense the uneasiness I felt that day in my stomach at the end of the presentation. It was more than gas! I gave my heart to Christ, and the course of my life has never been the same.

At one Vacation Bible School, I won a new fishing pole when I memorized more verses than any other student in my class. I am still thankful for the short ones like John 11:35, "Jesus wept," because it was a full verse and counted just like the long ones did. Oh, and there was one special VBS where I met my first girlfriend and got to see her every day! Of course, I was only in the seventh grade, when having a girlfriend was a beautiful thing.

This week, Zach is helping with a Children's Day Camp program at Central Baptist Church in Bearden, our home church in Knoxville. It is fulfilling to see your own children passing down the great legacy and tradition of caring for the needs of young people. Central Baptist of Bearden is trying something different this year. Instead of having one big Vacation Bible School at the church with hundreds of kids in attendance, they are hosting regional VBS meetings all over the city of Knoxville in various locations. Dr. Harold Bryson is hosting the adults at the church while teaching the book of Revelation and has had over 350 adults come for his study throughout the summer. Vacation Bible School is alive and well—even for the grownups.

Zach came home the first night while helping with the program and said, "Working with the kids is a lot of fun." He told the story about a little boy who had never been away from home for any length of time by himself. Zach said he did great until a girl came up and started a conversation, and he literally went to pieces and started crying uncontrollably! It reminded me of one of my first times in charge of a summer VBS program for children. I was serving as a part-time youth pastor in Oklahoma my senior year of college. The children were fun, and I learned a lot from that experience. I will never forget taking two little brothers for a ride in a red wagon on the parsonage lawn. I started to speed up and took a turn way too sharp. Both siblings tumbled out onto the lawn in a roll. Their mother was standing guard a few feet away. I felt *so bad*! But she was gracious. I picked up the boys, put them back in the wagon, and started out again—this time very cautiously!

I encourage you to support the Vacation Bible School here at the First Baptist Church of Bristol this summer. There will be something for people of all ages. Even if you are unable to help with the children, please come and be part of the Adult Bible Study. Dr. Gene Eller will be leading it once again, and he is a wonderful teacher. The Kool-Aid tastes even sweeter as an adult! And Joe Emmert does a wonderful job with our children's programs. Your presence will encourage him and others. Who knows? You may even have a little fun along the way. And I promise I will not be giving any wagon rides to young people; I learned my lesson well!

Hope to see you there!

28

The Gift of New Life

"You are with child" are blessed words. There are pronouncements of childbirth throughout the pages of the both the Old and New Testaments. Exodus 1:22–2:10 celebrates the birth of Moses and the quick thinking of Moses' mother and sister in preserving his young life. Ruth 4:13-17 recounts the birth of Obed and secures the ancestry of King David. Over and over again, we are told of the births of men and women who would accomplish great things in the biblical narrative. The New Testament includes two separate accounts of the birth of Jesus in Matthew 1:18-24 and Luke 2:1-7. In addition to the canonical Gospels, there are other writings called the Infancy Gospels that describe Jesus as a child and tell of his early years. Surely the words "you are with child" are a blessing from God.

For some, however, these are words of terror and shame. Throughout middle schools, high schools, and colleges, young women are often devastated to hear those words: "You are with child." "You are pregnant." A recent government study, using data from 2008, revealed that there were a total of 4,248,000 live births, 1,212,000 induced abortions, and 1,118,000 fetal losses in 2008. The estimated pregnancy rate for 2008 was 105.5 pregnancies per 1,000 women aged 15 to 44, which is about 9 percent below the 1990 peak, the new report showed. According to this study, 2008 statistics reported the lowest rate of teen pregnancy since 1976 (Denise Mann, *HealthDay News*, 12 June 2012). But even with this concerted drop in teen pregnancies, many young women face this uphill struggle alone without any real support.

As a body of believers, we have an obligation to extend the love of Jesus Christ to everyone. Our homes, our families, our church body, and certainly our larger community are not immune to the realities of children being born into less than ideal circumstances. What are we doing to help meet the physical and spiritual needs of this subset of our community? Another issue related to this social problem is the large number of grandparents who are becoming full-time caregivers for their grandchildren.

My brief word of encouragement for you today is a call to do two things. First, I ask you to pray for every young woman who hears those words this week: "You are with child." Mothers who are in loving, marital relationships also need our prayers. In the chaos of our world today, it is not easy being a wife, mother, and often a career woman. Pray as well for unwed mothers today. They especially need to know that someone cares about them and the well-being of their soon-to-be-born child. Second, I urge you to help young mothers who are around you in your daily life. Simple things like providing temporary childcare can be such a huge help in the life of a young mother. Volunteering to watch a little one for a young couple with a newborn can be such a blessing and doesn't cost a thing except your time. If you have the means, the purchase and gifts of diapers, formula, and extra clothing can also be helpful to young families.

When both Brack and Zachary were in day care at the same time I used to call them my Mercedes babies. Kim and I literally could have been making the monthly payments on a high-end Mercedes for what we were paying each month in day care, diapers, and formula. This must be doubly difficult for single parents.

I encourage you to keep your eyes open to the many ways you can make a difference. The love and relationship that we enjoy with Jesus Christ wasn't meant only for us and our families. We are called to go beyond the walls of the church building and beyond the walls of our insular homes and be the hands and feet of Jesus Christ to a lost and broken world. Caring for young mothers and their dear, sweet children is just one way we can live out the faith that we share.

29

Life Is Fragile

What is your life? You are a mist that appears for a little while and then vanishes. (James 4:14, NIV)

A heartfelt thank you is due to all of you who have called, emailed, texted, and asked about our families who live in Oklahoma and have endured unspeakable tragedies over the past two weeks. The tornadoes that swept through the central part of the state have brought devastation and heartache.

My nephew Keaton watched from the top steps of his storm shelter as the tornado formed about a mile from his home and went northeast, traveling through Moore en route to killing twenty-four people that fateful day. Last Friday, the tornadoes that went through the southwest corner of Oklahoma City put my sister and her two boys once again on high alert. One of the tornadoes passed within just a few hundred yards of their home in Tuttle, Oklahoma. The death toll continues to rise from this latest outbreak of storms.

I learned on Monday that last Friday's storm claimed the life of one of my second cousins. He was traveling in his pickup to check on someone when the first tornado struck near El Reno. Tragedies come to us all.

These events remind us that life is fragile. The musician Sting reminds us of our fragility and our penchant for violence in his 1987 song, "Fragile."

For all those born beneath an angry star
Lest we forget how fragile we are
On and on the rain will fall
Like tears from a star, Like tears from a star
On and on the rain will say
How fragile we are, How fragile we are

Life is so fragile. But even in our vulnerability, we can live with purpose and meaning. We must not live in fear. We are to celebrate each day as another opportunity to live. We all can have purpose and meaning in living well. Living well means dedicating our hearts and lives to Jesus Christ and to his purposes. We are challenged to live in the service of others. We are to put the needs of others before our own. Life is fragile, but it is worth living. When we do for others, we help them realize the love of God in a world that teeters toward extinction each and every day. For some, that may come in the form of a violent storm or accident. For others, it may be the peaceful sense of sleep after a full and meaningful life. The end of life comes for us all. Let us celebrate each and every breath and fulfill the purposes for which we are created!

How fragile we are.

30

Life Is Broken

This week I would like to take another close look at the issue of life. Last week we visited the topic of life's fragility. Today, let's stop and consider the brokenness of life.

A couple of weeks ago, Kim and I had the joy of spending a few days at the beach. We spent much of our time walking up and down the surf, enjoying the sand and warm water washing away the cares of another successfully completed school year. On our walks, we always scour the beach looking for washed up jellyfish, starfish, and unusual shells. I brought back one particularly interesting shell. Small and shaped like a miniature conch shell, it was beautiful even though it was also battered. Many of its edges were broken off or chipped away. As I picked up the shell and placed it my pocket, it reminded me of the brokenness of life.

When we journey through the rigors of our daily lives, we sometimes become tossed around by the day-to-day struggles we encounter. We are chipped, frayed, and broken. Yet we are also beautiful. There is beauty in you that comes to the forefront, not through the ease of life, but rather through its brokenness.

Many in our church have suffered immensely throughout the years with various tragedies of life. Personal setbacks have befallen most of us over time. Illnesses and death have touched most of our families at one time or another. We are sometimes disappointed with those we consider friends and fellow church members. Sometimes the words said about us have pierced our innermost places. Failed business opportunities or lack of opportunity for personal advancement have beset many of us over the years. Yet there is a strange beauty. It is not in our perfection but squarely present in our brokenness.

Brokenness plays an important role in the teaching of Jesus. Both in his words and actions, Christ repeatedly used the issue of brokenness to communicate the truth of his message. When Jesus gathered followers for a meal, the Scriptures record that he took bread and broke it, blessed it, and distributed it for use. In this illustration, we see that brokenness is sometimes a condition or prerequisite in our lives before we can be properly used by God. Brokenness creates an opportunity for us to rely more heavily on our heavenly Father. When we are broken, we realize that any beauty, honor, or truth in our lives is not from us but is truly given from above.

In a far more vivid example, Jesus' body was broken for us during the experience of the trial and crucifixion so long ago. He was beaten, scourged, belittled, mocked, and dehumanized. God used the brokenness of Jesus to open the door to our gift of salvation—to the gift of becoming followers of Christ. To be a disciple of Christ today means that we are willing to suffer as Jesus suffered. We must be willing to offer ourselves as daily sacrifices before a world that is all too happy to mock, belittle, and dehumanize us each day. But I remind you, even as I remind myself, that it is precisely through that brokenness that we are transformed into the image of Christ.

Embrace your brokenness and embrace the brokenness of others. Though these words do not appear in this manner in the Beatitudes, they are nonetheless there in spirit: *Blessed are the broken, for they are being transformed into the image of God.*

I am praying for each of you as you consider God's direction.

31

Life Is Joy

Dear brothers and sisters, I love you and long to see you, for you are my joy and the reward for my work. (Paul in Philippians 4:1, NLT)

What a weekend!

Kim and I celebrated the wedding of our oldest son, Brack, in Garner, North Carolina, on Saturday. Brack and Courtney were glowing all throughout the long day that we call the wedding process: pictures, more pictures, preparations for the ceremony, the ceremony, the general reception, and then the private reception for close friends and family members. It was a long but blessed day! It was a rare privilege as a father and minister to have a part in the ceremony. On Sunday morning, Kim and I were driving with a family friend, Suzi Miller, to attend worship services at our former church home of Buies Creek First Baptist Church when we received an unexpected telephone call. Brack and Courtney were returning items before they went away and wanted to meet us for lunch at Lillington, North Carolina. It was a special treat to see them again so soon. Life is joy!

The wedding weekend was a special treat for our family. We had family members come from all across the country. Friends and family were there from the far-off lands of France and Japan. Friends from church fields we served in the past were present from North Carolina, Miami, Florida, Tennessee, Oklahoma, Cleveland, Ohio, and many other points in between. It was a large turnout and a fun occasion. It was difficult just to make sure I made it to most of my friends to thank them for coming. Life is joy!

Many of you have blessed us with your outpouring of love for Brack and Courtney during this season, and Kim and I would like to say a heartfelt thank you to every one of you! Your cards, letters, texts, emails, and gifts are greatly appreciated. Brack and Courtney move into a fully furnished two-bedroom apartment and are hitting the ground running with new jobs in Shelby, North Carolina. Brack also starts a Masters of Divinity program in the fall at the White Divinity School at Gardner-Webb University. Life is joy!

In the verse from Philippians, the Apostle Paul expresses how he feels about the people who comprise the church at Philippi. The relationships he enjoyed with this group of people were described as his joy and reward. In many ways, Paul was also an interim minister. He went from place to place, starting churches and also maintaining his relationships with those places where he served for brief periods. Paul describes throughout this letter how the Philippian congregation had helped meet many of his needs at various points in his ministry.

The First Baptist Church of Bristol has a new pastor! Woo hoo! On Sunday, I heard a collective shout and sigh of relief from every member of the pastor search committee all the way over in Eastern North Carolina. A few people of our congregation may not realize just how many hours and evenings are given in the process of leading a church to find a new leader. Kudos to our committee as we welcome Reverend Ronnie Brewer as the next pastor! Life is joy!

In a real way, you the First Baptist Church of Bristol have also been my joy and reward. You have continued to bless my family and me in so many ways. Your friendship, your encouragement, and your constant words of appreciation have been meaningful to us all. As we begin to prepare for what is ahead for our family, we simply pause today to say thank you for being so wonderful. You have helped us recharge our ministerial batteries, you have led us to heal from wounds that were fresh and piercing, and you have granted us one of the most important gifts any member can ever receive from a congregation: the gift of friendship. Life is joy!

Counting it all joy!

32

Life Is Worth Living

We, the members of First Baptist Church of Bristol, have received some difficult news in recent weeks. Many of you, our friends and families, have heard unpleasant words concerning medical issues and personal illnesses. When we visit our news outlets, we are bombarded with negative images and portrayals of humanity's cruelty to one another. We can feel like the author of Psalm 13, who cries out to God, "O LORD, how long will you forget me? Forever? How long will you look the other way?" (v. 1, NLT).

It is easy to come to a place of despair. We sometimes feel isolated, alone, and a long way from the loving embrace of our heavenly Father.

But I want to remind you today that life is worth living! Yes, there are struggles that await us. We all have our shares of trials, temptations, and wrong turns. There are also rainbows in our world. There are the smiles and giggles of babies who make us say such silly things. Who among us doesn't enjoy making a little "baby talk" once in a while?

Roller coasters, funnel cakes, and hot fudge Sundays remind us that life is worth living. Pivotal moments like the birth of a grandchild, a wedding, or a retirement dinner remind us that there are moments of joy in life. There are marathons to run, mountains to scale, and oceans to cross—all because life is worth living.

At the end of Psalm 13 in verses 5 and 6, the author of this brief psalm offers a wonderful affirmation of faith: "But I trust in your unfailing love. I will rejoice because you have rescued me. I will sing to the LORD because he has been so good to me" (NLT). Have all the problems providing the background to verse 1 of this psalm magically gone away? Are verses 5 and 6 written after a time of deliverance? Both of these are possible, but I choose to read verses 5 and 6 as an affirmation that is made before the author even knows the outcome of the vexing situation.

Life is worth living though all hell is breaking loose around us. Life is worth living when we receive tragic news about ourselves or others. Life is worth living even when we fall terribly short of the dreams or desires we set for ourselves.

Life is worth living because of the One who holds life in his hands. Life is worth living because every breath is a gift from God. And in life, there is always hope that through each breath God is going to do something amazing. Sometimes God brings amazing things to life through our strength. But often God brings amazing things to life through our weaknesses. God works through our infirmities, frailty, and suffering to bring life to the world around us.

To my dearest brothers and sisters in Christ who are the recipients of such terrible news in your life in recent days, know that I truly hurt with you and cry with you concerning news that is so scary and frightening. But please know that, as one who has also suffered greatly, I truly believe that even through suffering, life is worth living! You are never alone.

Birthplace of Country Music Museum
Photo by Ben J. Butler

Guitar at Volunteer and State Street in front of Chamber of Commerce building
Photo by Ben J. Butler

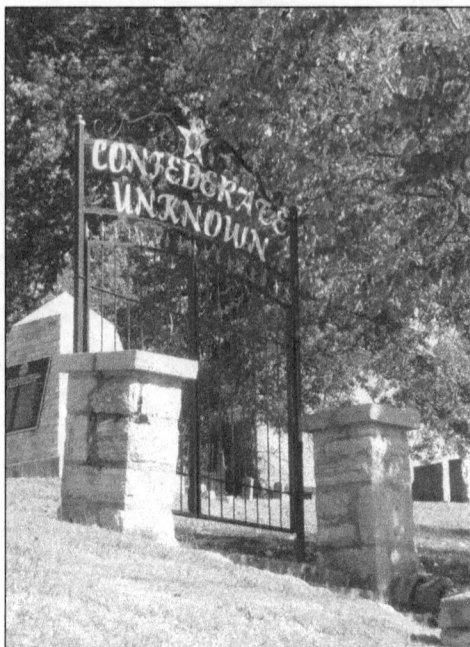

Entrance to Confederate section of East Hill Cemetery

Photo by Ben J. Butler

Historic East Hill Cemetery on East State Street

Photo by Ben J. Butler

First Baptist Church sanctuary built in 1912

Photo by Ben J. Butler

Restored building now used as Foundation Event Facility

Photo by Ben J. Butler

Historic Burger Bar at Piedmont and State Street. Voted best burger in VA in 2014.
Photo by Ben J. Butler

Coming together through Faith

33

Spring Is in the Air

Arise, my love, my fair one, and come away; for now the winter is past, the rain is over and gone. The flowers appear on the earth; the time of singing has come, and the voice of the turtledove is here in our land. The fig tree puts forth its figs, and the vines are in blossom; they give forth fragrance. Arise, my love, my fair one, and come away. (Song of Songs 2:10b-13, NRSV)

The emergence of spring is an amazing thing to witness each year. This year seems especially vibrant. One reason spring is so welcome this year is that winter seemed to keep its hold on us longer than usual. The weather appeared to be affecting my ability to effectively teach classes at Carson-Newman as well. A general mood of fatigue, depression, and malaise was the norm in my classes among college students this semester. We had a week off for spring break a couple of weeks back, but the weather prevented us from enjoying the outdoors. I found myself feeling jealous of some of my students and my own son, who were able to make it to warmer climates like the South Carolina or Florida beaches. I did, however, manage to cut wood and clean brush from some natural areas on our property. So the break wasn't a total loss.

But then—*wham*—here it is. Our first 80-degree day, and it is absolutely beautiful. The smiles are back. There are skips in our steps and light in our eyes. The birds seem more cheerful in their daily melody. The squirrels are feistier, the horses are more playful, and the wasps are making their annual reappearance. And yes, even college students, actually smiling in class, have an extra step in their giddy-up.

It is interesting what a difference that bright orb in the sky can make in our outlook for the day. We look forward to outdoor activities like golfing, hiking, waterskiing, working in flowerbeds and gardens, swimming, biking, and all the other "-ings" we can imagine.

In a similar way, when we commit ourselves to being followers of Jesus Christ, the sun is able to shine in our inner world. Spring arrives in our hearts. We experience an inner beauty and peace that can only be described as the presence of God. Many people we encounter each day seem to represent continuous winter by their demeanor and countenance. Many of them have never truly experienced the beauty of the sunshine that arrives in the spring, made possible through faith in Christ.

Take a moment today and simply look in a mirror. What season is reflected by your countenance? Are you cold and rainy, damp and dreary, moldy and wet? Or does your countenance reflect the presence of Jesus Christ? Can others see the ray of hope and confidence that overflows from us when Jesus Christ is Lord of our lives? There are four seasons for a reason. We generally reflect all the seasons throughout the course of a day and the course of our lives. But I urge you to try to allow the sun to shine in your heart. Without you and the light that Jesus Christ brings, there is little hope for our world but to be a cold, damp, dreary place. But, through faith in Christ, spring is in the air!

Let your light shine!

34

The Carrot Principle

The Carrot Principle was published by the Free Press in 2007. The subtitle is descriptive of the contents of the publication: *How the Best Managers Use Recognition to Engage Their People, Retain Talent, and Accelerate Performance.* The book is yet another offering in a long line of management trade books available in any popular bookstore, but the premise is somewhat different. Adrian Gostick and Chester Elton—members of the O.C. Tanner Group, a firm that specializes in leadership development—remind the reader of the importance of a well-placed "thank you."

The book focuses on the need for organizations and companies to do a better job of recognizing their employees. The authors stress the need for ongoing recognition rather than just a slip of paper and a slap on the back at the common five-, ten-, or twenty-year increments. For example, many companies do not even recognize the existence of new employees until they have served a minimum of five years with the company. Noting the research and data taken from the Jackson Organization, which specializes in survey and information gathering, the authors suggest that most employees have decided within the first two to three years if they are willing to continue their employment with an organization. Therefore, the five-year cutoff is way too late for a manager or employer to provide needed and wanted feedback. Gostick and Elton suggest beginning the process of employee recognition and appreciation on the very first day!

The authors also describe two different types of people who offer recognition to their employees. The first type is described as the "Expector." This type recognizes those who serve under them, but they always have ulterior motives in mind. They only give recognition when they expect that they too will receive something from the experience. The second type of recognizer is called the "Altruist." The Altruist gives recognition and praise because it is the right thing to do, not because of any personal gain or profit he or she can make from the process.

The "carrot principle" is that recognition and praise can make any organization or institution better. With this in mind, I would like to share a few practical suggestions and comments about the need for the "carrot principle" in our churches as it applies to our daily lives.

We can all live the "carrot principle" here at the First Baptist Church of Bristol. It is the art of saying a timely "thank you" for a job well done. We do not have to be in a position of management or leadership to express our appreciation for others. Last week, Zach Muncey, a former student of mine who has spent the last two years teaching English in China, surprised me with a lunch of shredded pork nachos from his workplace in Knoxville. He was in Jefferson City and just stopped by to deliver a wonderful lunch. It was a kind, thoughtful act. Those nachos may have been the best I have ever eaten!

Almost ten years ago, I had the opportunity to teach for the first time in St. Petersburg, Russia. I spoke no Russian at all and had to work solely through an interpreter. The first word I learned of my new Russian vocabulary is perhaps the most important—*spiceeba* (my poor transliteration), which means "thank you." Little things matter, and even when we do not speak the language, a genuine "thank you" translates into every tongue.

In Luke 17 we read the story of ten lepers who were healed by Jesus. Only one of them returned to say "thank you." I encourage you today to do something extraordinary and be the one of the ten who expresses appreciation for others. It will make all the difference.

35

The Schilling Tendon Procedure

In 2004, Curt Schilling, a right-handed starting pitcher for the Boston Red Sox, made two of the gutsiest outings in Major League Baseball history. On October 19, 2004, Schilling was the winning pitcher while facing the New York Yankees in game 6 of the series, forcing a game 7. At the end of the game, Schilling's sock was covered in blood due to the bleeding of his sutures following surgery to repair a tendon injury in his ankle. His effort led the Red Sox in coming back from three games down to win the series. Boston was the first team ever to come back and win after being three games down in a playoff series. They went on to the World Series and beat the St. Louis Cardinals with four straight wins.

Following the win against the Yankees, Schilling threw away his bloody sock at Yankee stadium. The second bloody sock, following the Cardinals game in the World Series, found its way to Cooperstown and was exhibited in the Baseball Hall of Fame. A few years ago, on the way to spend a week in Maine, my family and I visited Cooperstown and I got to see the famous "bloody sock." It was amazing to be a witness to one of the most amazing feats of an athlete playing through obvious pain and injury.

This weekend, you and I were witness to another amazing feat that is no less remarkable than what Schilling achieved, and it took place at the cantata at the First Baptist Church of Bristol.

Kim has had some physical ailments that were not easily diagnosed, and she didn't seem to be getting better. She was able get in to see an ear, nose, and throat specialist who started her on a journey to discover the source of her ongoing ailment. On Thursday of last week, following some tests, it was discovered that Kim has two "significant" tumors on her thyroid glands and faces surgery to remove these tumors. Kim had a big decision to make. Should she try to sing, even though she can barely breathe or swallow, or should she rest her voice? For those of you who were there, you witnessed that she did not rest her voice. Kim sang beautifully. Like Curt Schilling, she wasn't 100 percent; there have been many performances that were more memorable and breathtaking. But none of those earlier performances were nearly so amazing! Thank you, Kim, for being a wonderful wife, a phenomenal mother, and an inspiration in your service to Christ.

Congratulations to the choir, the musicians, Dr. Zembower, and Eric and Angie for a memorable worship experience. It was a great event for everyone at the First Baptist Church.

Postscript: What began as a cancer scare for Kim turned out to be a diseased thyroid. She had successful surgery to remove her thyroid and has made a complete recovery. Her voice never fully recovered, but she is back in full health once again, and for this we are eternally grateful. Thank you to everyone for your kind words of encouragement during and after the cantata.

36

God Provides
(The Lord Will See to It)

When is the last time you were in genuine, earnest prayer before God? A number of things in life keep us in the proverbial prayer closet. Emergencies come in many different forms. The timely emergencies before us keep us humble, and they are a call for us to live in a continuous state of daily prayer.

We are reminded frequently about God's provisions in Genesis 22:14. Here God gave the sacrificial lamb to replace Abraham's son Isaac, whom he was about to offer as a sacrifice. The New Living Translation reads, "Abraham named the place Yahweh-Yireh [which means "the Lord will provide"]. To this day, people still use that name as a proverb: 'On the mountain of the Lord it will be provided.'"

The Hebrew in this passage is best transliterated as *Adonai Yireh*. The first word, *Adonai,* is a substitute word for the Tetragrammaton, the four letters of the divine name, which was never to be uttered according to early Israelite religion and custom. We transliterate these letters as YHWH. The German spelling of the Tetragrammaton became better known as JHVH, and thus the name "Jehovah" was born. Though never a Hebrew word used for God, it has become popularized throughout Christendom as Jehovah. The devout Jewish person will never use this word because it is an attempt to speak the name of God audibly, and the name is not to be uttered aloud. The *Adonai* (Lord) or *Hashem* (the name) is always spoken aloud when a Jewish person reads from the Hebrew Bible and substitutes either of these two words for the four letters of the divine name.

The second word, *Yireh*, is taken from the root that means "to see." It is a verb form, and together with the Tetragrammaton it literally reads, "the LORD will see to it." This reference to seeing the place of God's provision is important in Genesis 22. In verse 2, God tells Abraham to take Isaac to a place that God will show him. God will give Abraham eyes to see this place. Thus, *Adonai Yireh* can indeed mean, "God will provide," but perhaps a closer translation here is simply to say, "God will see to it."

When we consider the numerous needs we encounter in the course of our daily lives, it is a great reminder that God is indeed still active in our world. No matter how great the needs, "God will see to it."

Paul writes of God's provisions for his needs and the needs of the early church in his letter to the Philippians. Philippians 4:19 states, "And this same God who takes care of me will supply all your needs from his glorious riches, which have been given to us in Christ Jesus" (NLT). Paul has been praising the Christians at Philippi because they have faithfully supported him by giving to his ministry. Paul thanks them for their ongoing support even when others had not helped in the same fashion. Through his prayer and blessing at the end of the letter, Paul encourages the Philippians to rely on the promise that God will provide for their needs.

The next time you are headed for the prayer closet because of the latest emergency or problem in your life, remember Philippians 4:19 and trust that God is faithful to meet all your needs—no matter how great, no matter how small. Jesus Christ cares for us and walks each day by our side. It's too bad for us, though, because on some days we simply forget that he is there!

Whatever your need, call on the name of Jesus Christ, and God will see to it!

37

Unceasing Prayer

Seven-year-old George let out with a loud, shrill whistle during the minister's prayer one Sunday. After church, his mother scolded him and asked, "Son, whatever made you do such a thing?" "I asked God to teach me to whistle, and he did just then," answered the boy.

Today, I want to share with you a Bible verse that can make a difference in your life. "Pray without ceasing" (1 Thess 5:17, KJV). "Pray continually" (NIV).

This passage is Paul's final exhortation to the Thessalonian church in this letter. Unceasing prayer implies five things.

1. A Devotional Spirit. Paul calls the Thessalonians to walk with God. To pray without ceasing is to walk constantly with God. Genesis 5:21-24 reminds us that Enoch walked with the Lord for 365 years, and then God took him up. A devotional spirit is an attitude that allows God to accompany you in your everyday activities.

With God (Author Unknown)
To talk with God no breath is lost: Talk on.
To walk with God no strength is lost: Walk on.
To toil with God no time is lost: Toil on.
Little is much, if God is in it:
Man's busiest day is not worth God's minute.
Much is little everywhere
If God the business doth not share.
So work with God, then nothing's lost
Who works with Him does well and most.
To pray without ceasing is to constantly walk with God.

2. A Life of Spontaneous Prayer. It can be a normal thing to talk to God spontaneously about life's concerns. I spent the summer of 1982 in Spain and will never forget the fervency of the young Spanish Christians and the way they prayed. They took Paul's exhortation to heart. It can look a little strange to pray while driving down the freeway, but wherever you are you can talk to God! By praying without ceasing, we keep our thoughts and minds on Christ.

3. Perseverance in Prayer. We should not stop praying until our prayers are answered. Romans 12:2 says, "Do not conform any longer to the pattern of this world, but be transformed by the renewing of your mind." Ephesians 6:18 states, "And pray in the Spirit on all occasions with all kinds of prayers and requests. With this in mind, be alert and always keep on praying for all the saints." In Luke 18:1 we read, "Then Jesus told his disciples a parable to show them that they should always pray and not give up." The parable was Jesus' tool to teach his disciples to have perseverance in their praying. How often have you started to pray for something or someone only to eventually give up after a short time? We must pray with perseverance!

4. Regular Prayer. We need to set aside segments of time each day to pray. Preferably, we should establish times when we can be alone, allowing ourselves a chance to escape from the hustle and bustle of the world. Colossians 4:2 says, "Devote yourselves to prayer, being watchful and thankful." Scripture records that many of the spiritual giants of the Bible kept regular times of prayer each day: David, Daniel, Shadrach, Meschach, and Abednego. Jesus also woke up early to go and pray.

5. A Spirit of Thanksgiving. We should pray with an attitude of thanksgiving for the prayers that are answered. God not only listens to your prayers but also answers them! Do you pray believing that your prayer will be answered? You can pray with thanksgiving when you fully trust that God will answer your prayers. "Prayer can truly be 'without ceasing' in the heart which is full of the presence of God, and evermore commencing with Him" (author unknown).

Keep praying. Please don't stop praying just because our Fall Renewal Services have come to a close. Prayer makes a difference in your life as a believer and in the life of our church. One of the most important aspects of renewal and vitality of the First Baptist Church of Bristol depends on our willingness to commit ourselves to the ministry of prayer.

Praying for you!

38

I Am a Heinz 57 and That's Okay

February is becoming famous for its designation as African-American History Month. The contributions of numerous African Americans to our society have been devalued for much too long. For every George Washington Carver, Booker T. Washington, Rosa Parks, or Martin Luther King, Jr., there are hundreds of other African-Americans who have made significant contributions in relative anonymity. May we all celebrate together the contributions of worthy individuals regardless of race, creed, or other differences.

Each of us should celebrate our diverse heritage. We all have the right and privilege to be proud of our individual backgrounds. Our experiences help bring unique perspectives and insights into our communities.

My own family history is a genealogist's worst nightmare. There have been major grafts of various nationalities into my family tree. My father is a descendant of French Colonials and Native Americans. The Ballard family is proud of our Cherokee bloodline. I am an active member of the Western Cherokee Tribe, participating in tribal elections and activities. My father's business in Oklahoma is federally recognized as a Native-American business.

My mother is a descendant of the Henderson clan from Scotland. Her family took part in the great land rush of 1889 in Oklahoma. The Henderson clan has a rich tradition in Scottish history. It was a Henderson who helped pen the first written language in Scotland. A Henderson is credited with first recording the story of William Wallace, who was portrayed in the movie *Braveheart*.

The confluence of a diverse ethnicity and tradition is part of who I am. In canine terms, I suppose you could call me a "Heinz 57." In a great melting pot like the United States of America, a "Heinz 57" is not so bad! Those like me stand as a living testimony that people from various places around the world can live together as friends and even as family.

Each of us should celebrate our commonality. We should take civic pride as citizens of our various towns, counties, and states. Our common goals include provision for our families, a future for our children, and a glimmer of hope for the generations yet to come.

Our commonality is a central part of the Christian tradition. Paul says in Galatians 3:26-28 that we are all the same through Jesus Christ: "You are all sons of God through faith in Christ Jesus, for all of you who were baptized into Christ have been clothed with Christ. There is neither Jew nor Greek, slave nor free, male nor female, for you are all one in Christ Jesus."

Some theologians have suggested that God is "colorblind." It is true that in the eyes of God we are all equals in Christ. Likewise, God created us as unique individuals. Our color is part of our unique individuality. God is not "colorblind." God sees us as we are, and God loves each of us as we are! Let us celebrate our individuality and commonality. May our communities reflect the kingdom of God with room for all races, creeds, and other differences—yes, even those of us who may be a "Heinz 57."

Till Death Do Us Part

39

I recently wrote a brief column on marriage, offering a traditional understanding of marriage as a commitment between a man and a woman for life in a relationship of mutual partnership and respect. Sometimes, however, those who have suffered through difficult marriages or abusive relationships can feel lessened because their marriage or relationship did not work out. They can feel like personal failures because their marriages ended in a divorce or their relationships ended poorly. Please allow me to clarify that I do not believe a spouse should have to endure constant abuse or domestic violence from a partner. Nor do I believe that, if your marriage or relationship ended poorly, your spiritual life has somehow ended and you are now a second-class believer. No marriage is perfect. But I truly believe that God is not honored when people endure abuse in a marriage because they argue that their partners have not been unfaithful.

According to the Department of Justice, domestic violence is defined as "a pattern of abusive behavior in any relationship that is used by one partner to gain or maintain power and control over another intimate partner. Domestic violence can be physical, sexual, emotional, economic, or psychological actions or threats of actions that influence another person. This includes any behaviors that intimidate, manipulate, humiliate, isolate, frighten, terrorize, coerce, threaten, blame, hurt, injure, or wound someone" ("Domestic Violence," http://www.ovw.usdoj.gov/domviolence.htm).

Christians often point to the passage in the New Testament that says divorce is allowed only in the case of infidelity. Matthew 5:31-32 states, "You have heard that the law of Moses says, 'A man can divorce his wife by merely giving her a letter of divorce.' But I say that a man who divorces his wife, unless she has been unfaithful, causes her to commit adultery. And anyone who marries a divorced woman commits adultery" (NLT). It is my understanding that Jesus is confronting a common practice by fellow members of the Jewish faith in his day. Some were apparently "putting away" their wives for as little as making a bad bowl of soup!

An elderly television evangelist made national headlines when he sort of chuckled at a wife who had called in to his program asking for help with a husband who had been unfaithful to her. The evangelist dismissed her pain by excusing the husband's actions, saying, "He's just a man." This type of response is most unfortunate and irresponsible in the church!

Marriages sometimes end in divorce. Other people live in abusive marriages every day. If you find yourself in a position where your marriage has ended, or you are being abused, please know that God still loves you. Most important, no one should have to live with daily abuse. There is help and hope for you.

If you know someone who is enduring abuse, I encourage you to reach out as a believer in Christ and love that person. We must offer the love of Jesus Christ to all who are hurting in our world. And in today's world, there are a staggering number of people who live with abuse every day.

Wishing God's best in your relationships.

Who Is in Charge?

40

In an article in the *Chronicle of Higher Education* (14 January 2013), Dennis Barden describes the plight of American colleges and universities as they seek new presidents to lead their institutions. Barden is a senior vice president with Witt/Kieffer, an executive search firm specializing in searches for academic and administrative leaders in higher education.

Barden describes the difficulty involved in identifying leaders who will be successful in executive leadership in higher education. He cites the firing of the leader of the University of Illinois system because he was too demanding and autocratic in his leadership style. This was contrasted with the dismissal and eventual rehiring of Teresa Sullivan, the president of the University of Virginia, because she was too deliberate in consensus building and thus slow in decision making. Barden asks the difficult question: What is a leader to do?

The article suggests three qualities of leaders who eventually succeed in landing the elusive post of executive leadership in higher education. (1) These leaders emit a level of energy and intensity that simply outpaces their competitors. (2) These leaders project a winning personality that elicits hope for happy and enjoyable relationships, which optimistically projects into successful fundraising. The most important quality according to Barden, however, is (3) the expressed willingness and desire to make tough decisions and live with the consequences. Barden sees these three qualities as necessary for success in leadership in higher education administration.

A year has passed. For many it has been a long year. For some it may have passed rather quickly. The First Baptist Church of Bristol has been without a full-time pastor for over a year. At times like these, fears can come to mind. When are we going to find someone to come and lead us? Does anyone want to be part of our fellowship? What kind of leader do we need to fill the pulpit and carry the mantle of leadership? As I did last Wednesday evening at our Bible study, I offer this advice once again: simply exhale and take a deep breath. We are going to be fine. There is no need to panic. It is far better to be careful in finding the leader that God is preparing rather than simply settling for the first person in sight.

I suggest that you apply the same principles Barden describes for leaders of positions in higher education. May we seek someone who is filled with energy for the task at hand. May we seek someone who is personable and who emits warmth, becoming a blanket of confidence for others. Finally, I pray that God leads our search committee to someone who relishes making the tough decisions and is not afraid to live with the consequences. Of course, I would add that all these things should be brought together under the Lordship of Jesus Christ.

Until that day comes, let me once again say thanks to you for the real joy it is to serve as your interim pastor. Kim and I have been blessed by your support and friendship. Kim wishes me to express our gratitude for your cards, thoughts of love, and phone calls over the past few weeks.

May you continue sharing the love of Christ in a broken world.

41

Searching
for Answers

I recently presented a chapel address at Carson-Newman University that was one message in a four-part presentation titled "Job: Suffering of the Soul." President Randall O'Brien, Don Garner, Bill Blevins, Carolyn Blevins, and I each gave one chapel address as part of this series. I am donating a copy of the series to the library of First Baptist Church of Bristol. I encourage you to check it out and watch the four presentations. An excerpt from my presentation is below. May the Lord bless you in the midst of the sufferings and joys that life can bring.

In Job 28, we find Job and with his three friends Eliphaz, Bildad, and Zophar engrossed in a heated debate over their question at hand: Why is Job suffering so greatly? Many Old Testament scholars describe this dialogue as the "Friends Cycle" in Job. In this cycle, Job entertains the assertions of Eliphaz, Bildad, and Zophar and then responds to their challenges. This happens three different times in Job 4–31. The cycle runs out of steam in Job 25 as we see Bildad only offering six verses on the third pass through, and Zophar is apparently on empty, as he is quiet on the third pass.

Throughout this cycle, the three friends bitterly defend traditional orthodox Retribution Theology, also known as Deuteronomic Theology. It is as if each one of the friends simply says, "Come on, Job, what did you do? Just confess, confess, confess; God is merciful and God will forgive you."

There is much scholarly debate concerning Job 28. At issue is the question of who is speaking in this chapter. In Job 26 and 27 we see Job responding to Bildad as part of the cycle of larger dialogue. In Job 29:1, however, we read, "Job continued his discourse" (NIV), suggesting perhaps that Job 28 was an interruption to Job's earlier soliloquy. Some scholars maintain that this poem about the mining of wisdom is foreign to the original story and text of Job, believing instead that it was included because of its unique wisdom language and message.

Our quest for answers in life ultimately takes each of us on a journey, much like Homer's legendary character, Ulysses, in *The Odyssey*. In Job 28 this journey is described in three stages.

In Job 28:1-11, the author suggests that our search for answers is like that of miners who search the earth for precious metals. They work diligently to find these metals that are deemed valuable: silver and gold in verse 1, iron and copper in verse 2, and then sapphires in verse 6, along with gold dust and gold nuggets. It is amazing that these precious jewels are still rare and desired commodities that many people spend all their time and energy searching for.

The author of Job 28 seems to be hinting that working for the treasures of this world is often humanity's answer to the mysteries of life. We can find precious metals if we are willing to dig deep enough, but who can find wisdom?

Jesus encountered those who sought only riches and responded with the words known today as Matthew 16:26: "What good will it be for a man if he gains the whole world, yet forfeits his soul? Or what can a man give in exchange for his soul?" (NIV)

In Job 28:12-22, the author continues to ask the reader to ponder where answers to our questions can be found. The author once again reminds us that life is much more than the accumulation of wealth and worldly treasures. Gold we can find. Silver we can dig for. But in verse 20 we hear the questions, "Where does wisdom come from? Where does understanding dwell?"

A firm affirmation is present in Job 28:23-28. The answer for many of the questions we seek rests only in the heart of God. Verse 23 records, "God understands the way to it [wisdom] and he alone knows where it dwells" (NIV).

We must take comfort in knowing that what we consider unanswerable may indeed have an answer. The great mysteries of this world and our lives are in plain view to the eyes of God.

Job 28:28 reminds us that we have access to the mysteries of life through our faith and trust in our Creator: "And he said to man, 'The fear of the LORD—that is wisdom, and to shun evil is understanding'" (NIV).

In the midst of our search for answers, we are encouraged to fear God and turn aside from that which is evil.

We will probably never know the answers for many of our pressing questions in life. We must take heart, however, that even though we may not find those answers, we can have a relationship with someone who understands our struggle and search for understanding. God cares for us enough to allow us to struggle, to question, and to yearn for answers to the unanswerable—all the while calling for us to live with hope, faith, and trust in God's care for our lives.

From a fellow sufferer.

42

How Do We Know?
(Part 1)

A few years ago, one of my students asked me a very good question concerning the Psalms of the Old Testament. The student asked how we can possibly consider the book of Psalms as the Word of God when the Psalms are filled with the cries of people who are crying out to God for help in their personal and collective lives?

This raises two important questions for us to consider today. How can we be sure that the voice we are listening to is that of God? How can we honestly and with integrity claim to know God's will for our lives or for the decisions we make?

Challenge: Answer these two questions in a way that can have some bearing on our lives today. Challenge accepted!

I reminded the student that God speaks in a number of ways. Yes, even in the words of ancient cries from people to God in times of distress. This collection of hymns, prayers, and cries that many people have expressed to God indicate that God has been in the business of listening to and answering prayers for a long time!

The Bible contains many types of literature. Some texts may not speak directly to issues we can relate to today. But I believe that ALL OF IT is God's Word. These words have been received by communities of faith, both Jewish and Christian, for over two thousand years. These separate faith communities have treated these words as sacred texts and as God's Word.

The Bible must have a prominent place in our lives and homes. It only becomes the Word of God when we choose to live out the principles recorded in this sacred writing. Life is breathed in the pages of God's Word through our lives, or it remains simply words on the page.

How can we be sure that we actually know God's will in our lives or in the life of the church? I start with my own assumption that God really wants us to know God's will. God's will is not some elusive, hidden plan that we have to find after making a dramatic or dangerous quest. God desires us to live our lives following God's direction for us. While God's will is often very simple, the problem many of us have is we want something else. Too often we simply ask God to bless our own course for our lives.

But how do we know? First, we must do what God has already shown us to do in our lives. I do believe that God is often waiting on us to see if we are really going to trust God before God gives us further instruction. We must be faithful in the tasks already before us, and then in God's timing God will make known the next step of the journey.

I am also convinced that sometimes God allows us to make those key choices in our lives to see where we are in our walk with God. Often we receive the feeling of confirmation or denial only after we make a decision.

Let me provide one example. Kim and I have been married for thirty years. We have always tried to honor God in our marriage and to do our best to follow God's will for our lives. When I finished the Masters of Divinity degree at Golden Gate Seminary, we had to decide what step to take next. I had looked at PhD programs and had been accepted to various programs and denied by others. Upon graduation we made the decision to move back to Oklahoma with the coming birth of our first son, and to aid in helping Kim's grandmother who was having hip replacement surgery.

While I was driving the U-Haul truck back to Oklahoma with my father and when Kim was flying back to Oklahoma we both had a similar experience. When I crossed the California border heading back East, I had a feeling deep inside that our decision was a mistake. Kim shared that she had the same feeling about the time she imagined the plane heading over the California/Arizona border towards Tulsa.

Was this the end? Was God through with us? Stay tuned next week as I continue our discussion on "knowing God's will" in our world today.

43

How Do We Know?
(Part 2)

The ever-elusive will of God is often the discussion of many forums and platforms. Theologians have debated this issue for centuries. Some Christian theologians believed that since God is omniscient (all-knowing) and immutable (unchanging), then our actions and decisions are all predetermined, and we are merely living out the actions or plans that have been arranged for us. I ended the previous article by outlining the story of Kim and me feeling like we had made a mistake in leaving California at that point in our married lives. According to those who hold to a predetermined direction, Kim and I were either wrong in our feelings or wrong in our actions; but these events were already set in motion, and we were simply playing out what we were destined to do.

Kim and I did not make the decision to leave California in a whimsical fashion. We prayed about it for some time. We discussed the benefits and costs of staying on the West Coast. We finally decided that family was more important at that time than our individual circumstances. First, Kim's grandmother needed someone to care for her during recovery from hip replacement surgery, and we were the most readily available within her family for such a mission. Second, we needed a place where we could be loved and supported in bringing a new life into the world. What better place than with family? Third, we felt like the San Francisco Bay Area was not the best place to raise children at that time. So off we went!

Yet we both felt like we made the wrong choice after the choice was made and the events of moving were in motion. We did not know each other's feelings until after we both arrived back in Oklahoma after a lengthy trip. After talking it over and reflecting on the move, we both confessed that we had felt similarly before our move, but neither one of us spoke up. We agreed never to repress such feelings again, but that we would speak up whenever we felt differently about a decision for our family.

If we believed in blind determinism, then we would have to admit that we had probably made the biggest mistake of our lives. But I praise God that God is bigger than a one-size-fits-all blueprint that has only one path we can take to follow him. In fact, I believe that God has not set our paths before us in stone. I believe that God walks with us, helping us each along our paths. God is able to take our daily choices and lead us in the way that God would have us to go. This happens through the relationship we have with Jesus Christ. And from my own experience, I believe that God uses our personal choices and experiences for God's kingdom. God is more concerned with the willingness of our hearts to follow him than with any secret course that some believe may be predetermined in our lives.

So relax and trust in the ability of God to guide, direct, and help us get back on course when we stray. God has gifted each of us in unique ways, and we are placed in varied locations at varied times to bring about God's purposes in the world around us. There was only one Abraham, only one Moses, only one David, and only one Jesus. There is also only one you, and God has given you all the gifts and endowment of God's Spirit you need to complete God's task for your life each day. When we open ourselves to God's leading, God can use us in a myriad of ways to make a difference in our world. Especially when we feel like we may have erred, God is there to pick up the pieces of our lives and create something special for God's kingdom!

**Rhythm & Roots annual September music event,
which draws thousands to Bristol's State Street**

Photo by Bristol Rhythm and Roots

Relief art on Quaker Steak building
Photo by Ben J. Butler

Quaker Steak & Lube (motor-themed restaurant)
Photo by Ben J. Butler

Auto Race Mural on State Street
Photo by Ben J. Butler

**Rhythm & Roots sign for annual September music event,
which draws thousands to Bristol's State Street**
Photo by Daniel Hardoby

The Paramount, an Art Deco theater built in 1931 and restored in 1991.
Photo by Bristol Rhythm and Roots

Seasons

44

Father's Day Once Again

It is that time of year once again. The rush is on to find the perfect card or the right gift, and to schedule that visit or call to our fathers sometime on Sunday.

I am grateful for my father. He was able to retire recently and seems to be enjoying the idea of setting his own schedule for a change.

Many in our world today have never experienced the joys of having a loving father. Regrettably, some children have suffered years of abuse and turmoil with a less than desirable father. Some children never know what it is like to have a father figure in their lives. My own father bounced around in foster care for most of his early years until a caring Christian family finally welcomed him into their home. He only saw his biological father one time before his father passed away. It was not the meeting that movies are made of. Even though my father never experienced love and nurture from his biological father, he committed himself to being a great father to his children. My early years were spent playing catch in the backyard, working with horses, and planting a garden—all as a family. My dad even built a baseball diamond in a corner of a field he owned in Shreve, Ohio. Kids from all over town would come and play baseball on my field! I am grateful for my father.

Of all the things my father did for me, perhaps the most important is the passing along of his core values. Core values guide us in our day-to-day decision making. The living out of these values determines who we are and ultimately determines our responses to the challenges we face in life. The first value that my father passed along was that of hard work. My father could easily be described as a workaholic. When he returned from his job, he immediately went to work around the gentleman's farm. He strongly rebuked us if we ever stood around with our hands in our pockets while others were engaged in work. There was rarely a Saturday morning when I got to sleep in. Saturday was just another unpaid workday!

A second value my father passed along is the importance of the Christian faith in our home. If the church doors were open, we were there! Sunday morning, Sunday night, Wednesday evening, church workdays, revival meetings, and many more times in between, our family was at the church. Faith was an important part of our home. And for that I am most grateful.

Special occasions like Father's Day help us remember what is really important to us. A time of interim pastoral ministry can also be a special time in the life of a church. This interim time provides the opportunity for families of faith to revisit our core values as a body of believers. We have the time to ask ourselves, "What values are most important to us?" How do these values shape who we are and what we do each week? Sometimes we find that perhaps we are not effectively operating by the core values that we all share. I encourage you to review your core sense of values—as individuals and as a body of believers. What values guide our path in our life of faith?

Happy Father's Day to all of the men in our fellowship!

45

Living Our Faith at Thanksgiving

This month I am focusing on the book of Jonah and its place in our Judeo-Christian canon. Jonah is one of my favorite books in the Hebrew Bible, and it holds a wealth of treasure for those who are willing to navigate its waters.

One of the primary themes of Jonah is its emphasis on God's love for all creation. In this story, God expresses care for the hated enemies of Israel, as well as for the animals of the land, the foreign sailors who took Jonah away from Joppa, and in a larger way for every created creature. My intent in looking at Jonah at this time is purposeful. November and December are months when it is easy to become myopic in our attention to ourselves and our immediate families.

The holiday season is a prime time for us as devoted followers of Christ to show the world a different way of celebrating the season. We have the opportunity to reach out when most everyone is looking inward. We have opportunities each day for outreach in a way that isn't present January through October. The word "holiday" is an abbreviated term from Holy Day. These days were meant to carry a tenor of reverence and awe. They were to be different, and thanksgiving and praise to God were to be part of these celebrations. There are many Holy Days mentioned in the narratives of Israel. Today they are national holidays in Israel, but they are also days to reflect and to worship God for his saving grace to God's people.

Yes, I love turkey, dressing, and football on Thanksgiving, but it is also a great time to volunteer at a homeless shelter, feeding the homeless and the less fortunate. It is also a great opportunity to share a moment of worship at your family's Thanksgiving table. Consider reading a text like Psalm 100, often called the "Old Thanksgiving," before you offer a word of thanks for the meal. It is a great time to be reminded of the blessings of God in our lives. As you are able, look for others in your sphere of life that you can invite to share with you in this great traditional meal. Do you know any foreign students who have no place to go during an American holiday? This is a great time to consider taking in the widow, the alien, or the orphan!

Outreach is an essential part of our call to discipleship. Why not take this wonderful annual opportunity to share the love of Jesus Christ in a tangible way with those around you? After all, Jonah is not just a children's story. It is the word of God for a lost and broken world teetering over a wrathful and restless ocean.

I would like to say a note of thanks today to everyone for your warm cards and gifts of appreciation during Pastor Appreciation Month. Your kindness is greatly appreciated and not taken for granted. Unfortunately, I have not had time yet to enjoy any of these extra treats, but I am looking forward to a time when I can enjoy them. Thanks again for everything. The plaque from the church will hold a special place in my home office. It is a real joy to serve with you as your interim pastor.

Blessings during this upcoming holiday season. May your holidays be Holy Days.

46

Are You Ready for Christmas?

Are you ready for Christmas? One could respond, I've got shopping to do, cooking to prepare, parties to attend, cameras and disks to buy, decorations to set in place, and the list can go on and on. One could also respond, Yes, I can't wait to see family and friends, to see the children on Christmas morning, to devour some goodies Mom or Grandma made this year, and to watch *It's a Wonderful Life* for the millionth time!

If the responses listed above sound familiar, then chances are you are not ready for Christmas. Preparing for Christmas has nothing to do with shopping, trimming, cooking, or long checkout lines. Let us begin to prepare for Christmas today as we consider the birthday of the Lord of lords and King of kings.

In Matthew 2:1-12 we read about travelers who come before the young Christ and offer special gifts to him. Matthew 2:11 lists the gifts of the magi. What did the magi do when they first encountered Christ? They fell down and worshiped, and they gave him presents!

The names Saphar, Melchior, and Balthasar are the legendary names given to the magi, yet Matthew does not give us an actual number of those present. The number three is suggested by the number of gifts, but we don't know how many were there. Matthew also records that the visit took place in a house (2:11) and not in a manger or cave as mentioned in Luke, though both Gospels name the city of Christ' birth as Bethlehem.

People often spiritualize the magi's gifts today. Many equate gold with royalty, frankincense with divinity, and myrrh with humanity. These gifts were not extraordinary in and of themselves, but were rather the expected gifts given to those of royal and acclaimed heritage.

For just a moment, I ask you to consider the central meaning of this presentation of gifts for the newborn king. Let us remember that these gifts represented the best these people could offer to a king. They did not offer their leftovers or second best items. I don't think the magi were "re-gifting" on that special day. Far too often, we offer only what is left over to Christ and Christ's service. I have often witnessed God's people treating the church and their giving to Christ's church as an afterthought, or they give only out of what was left over.

In your frenetic preparation for Christmas this year, let me suggest some gifts you could give this year:

Gift Ideas for Adults/Parents

1. Bring your family to church every Lord's Day in the new year.
2. Serve in a new capacity in church service or leadership in the new year.
3. Allow Jesus to be the Lord of your life every day in the new year.
4. Share Jesus with someone every week in the new year.
5. Love your spouse as Christ loved the church.
6. Encourage your spouse to be godly in all phases of life.
7. Be a model of Christian service to your entire family.
8. Pray daily for your family and their needs, both at home and at church.

Gift Ideas for Children and Teenagers

1. Be a consistent witness for Jesus in your school and at home.
2. Commit to memorize one verse of Scripture every week.
3. Respect your parents and school authorities even though you may disagree with them.
4. Share with a friend once a week what Jesus means to you.
5. Be grateful for the provision God has given to you through your parents.

Christmas is often a frantic time of year. The malls are packed with people trying to get the best deal or find that perfect gift. Many Christians treat their approach to Christ and Christmas as they do their Christmas shopping: *What can I get from this church or that church?* We have brought our shopper's mentality with us to church. The Christian faith isn't about how much I can *get* this Christmas, but rather what can I *give* to honor the birth of our Lord.

You are the most important gift you can give to Christ this Christmas. Are you ready for Christmas?

Merry Christmas.

47

Traditions

Christmastime is filled with rich traditions. As a small child I remember rushing down the steps in our home, all excited about tearing open Christmas presents, yet aware that my parents were very tired for some reason. They pleaded with us to sleep in but always to no avail. When my family moved from northern Ohio to rural Oklahoma, we developed new traditions. Every Christmas Eve, all my mother's brothers and sisters and their children gathered at my grandparents' home to celebrate together. Christmas Eve was my grandmother's birthday. She always spent her birthday money making sure that all her grandchildren (at least twenty-five of us) had new underwear, socks, or gloves. I miss the simplicity and the thoughtfulness of those special gifts! It is amazing that forty to fifty people could gather in a 1,000-square foot home, but we did. Some traditions are rich, and we cherish them.

On a few occasions I have had the honor of visiting the University of Salamanca in Spain. It is the oldest and most prestigious university in the Spanish-speaking world. It is the third oldest university in Europe that has been in continuous operation since its founding in 1134. The school received a royal charter from King Alfonso IX in 1218. The University of Salamanca was the first institution to be called a "university," achieving this title in 1254. Just visiting this historic place is a religious experience for any true academic. Columbus first pitched his case before the Royal Council of Geographers seeking a western route to the Indies in those hallowed halls. Another explorer, Hernan Cortez, also attended the school. St. John of the Cross, the famous theologian and Christian mystic, studied there. Of course, who could forget the author of *Don Quixote*, Miguel de Cervantes, who also studied at the University of Salamanca? Even today it remains the elite university in the Spanish-speaking world.

The University of Salamanca is filled with rich traditions. It was founded around a great Roman Catholic cathedral. The doctoral program at the university has some amazing traditions. The night before a doctoral candidate defends his or her dissertation, he or she is allowed to spend the night under the great cathedral in the catacombs. There is one particular vault where most students spend the night. It contains a full sarcophagus shaped in the outline of a human body. The students spend the night with a chair near the head of the sarcophagus and their feet propped on the head in order for the wisdom of the person buried in the chamber to be shared with the student. In Medieval times, if the student was successful in his or her defense, the family celebrated by throwing a huge party for the entire university and the surrounding town. If unsuccessful, the student was tarred and feathered, then run out of town. Another tradition for the successful doctoral student involves the cathedral. Upon successful completion of the doctoral defense, the student was given a bucket of bull's blood and allowed to write anything they wanted in blood on the outside walls of the cathedral. To this day, when you visit the great cathedral at Salamanca, you can see remnants of past writing in blood all over the exterior of the cathedral.

Please don't be alarmed; I didn't spend the night before my dissertation defense at the University of Tennessee with my feet on the head of a sarcophagus under the sanctuary at the First Baptist Church of Bristol. And I am certainly not going to take a bucket of bull's blood and write something profound on the outside of our beautiful sanctuary. But to celebrate my completing a PhD in Higher Education Administration at the University of Tennessee while I served as interim pastor here, I would like to pass along one of the traditions of the University of Salamanca. Kim and I would like to extend to you an invitation to a brief reception in Rosser Hall immediately following the Sunday morning worship service for light refreshments and fellowship. This is our way of saying thank you for your presence and words of encouragement, which have nourished our souls. Hope to see you there!

Thankful to God for all of you.

48

Ash Wednesday

This week is the beginning of the season of Lent. It is the time of preparation by the larger Christian community for the blessed Easter event. It is a time for prayer, fasting, and repentance. For the next forty days, many of our friends in various Christian traditions will give up various things as a way of purifying themselves and making lifestyle changes as Easter slowly approaches.

On Facebook I have already seen people saying they are giving up things like coffee or chocolate. One friend said she is giving up Facebook for Lent. Another wrote that he is giving up Facebook only on the weekends for Lent.

What are you giving up for Lent? Here are some suggestions to consider.

1. Let us give up living only for ourselves and always insisting on our way.
2. Let us give up talking poorly about others in any context because of the harm it can bring.
3. Let us give up treating people differently based on their socioeconomic status, dress, or appearance.
4. Let us give up the habit of regularly missing Sunday school and church worship services.
5. Let us give up the practice of only picking up the Bible on Sundays and neglecting to read from its pages throughout the week as well.
6. Let us give up expecting someone else to make that call, visit, or personal connection to a person that God has placed on our hearts.
7. Let us give up trying to handle life's care and stress alone.
8. Let us give up watching that television program or movie or listening to a song that we know does not honor Christ with its content.

9. Let us give up turning our backs on friends and neighbors that we think may not know Jesus Christ as their Lord and Savior.

10. Let us give up trying to determine our children's lives, or ultimately living through them, and allow God to be Lord of their lives as well.

These are some of the things we might consider giving up for Lent. In comparison, yes, chocolate, coffee, or Facebook might be much easier to give up than any of these things, but we would be better off as people and believers if we could give up even one or two of the things above that apply to our lives.

One of the great things about the Christian walk is that it is a voluntary experience. We are all on the journey as individuals. We are all on different stages of the journey that travels many different paths along the way. May each of us embrace the journey that is before us, under the Lordship of Jesus Christ, and endeavor to do our best to follow Christ each day in our homes, our places of employment, and our relationships.

May you have a blessed Lenten season.

Saying Goodbye

49

The end has finally come to my fast-paced fourteen-month run as your interim pastor. It has been a blast. Yesterday was very special. The kind words and gifts during the worship service, the fellowship and food at the luau, and of course all the well wishes throughout the day meant a lot to me. And I hope you still remember the three points from yesterday's message: Love One Another, Love One Another, and Love One Another.

This message seems so simple. Yet it is often so hard to live.

Dear friends, let us continue to love one another, for love comes from God. Any who loves is born of God and knows God. But anyone who does not love does not know God – for God is love. (1 John 4:7-8, NLT)

It really is that simple. When we act in love, we are living like Jesus Christ and pleasing our heavenly Father. When we do not act in love, we are not living like Jesus Christ and we are displeasing our heavenly Father. Loving one another is a choice we make each and every day. It takes work, but it is worth the effort. Some people are certainly harder to love than others, but we must make the effort no matter how difficult it is.

It has been my privilege to serve in several churches over the course of the past thirty-plus years I have been in the ministry. There have been real blessings in every stop along the way. But the friendships I have enjoyed with you have been truly unique and special. You have been a real blessing and encouragement to the inner parts of my being. I will dearly miss my weekly forays into the Bristol area. Thank you so much for everything you have done for my family and me.

Kim's solo yesterday was her first opportunity to sing publicly since having throat surgery back in January. We praise God for her recovery. Just a few weeks ago, Kim was not confident that her voice was fully returning.

I think it is safe to say she is going to be fine! Thank you so much for your prayers and words of support for her service as well.

Goodbye for now. Please know that I am praying for each of you, the church as a whole, and for your new pastor and family. I encourage you to support him and his family in the same manner you have cared for me and mine. Truly great things are in store for the First Baptist Church of Bristol.

In the name of Jesus,
Wayne Ballard

Street signs at State and Volunteer Streets. Volunteer Street goes south from this intersection into Tennessee, while Commonwealth goes north into Virginia.

Photo by Ben J. Butler

A plaque in State Street which marks the state line dividing Tennessee from Virginia.

Photo by Ben J. Butler

Bristol Train Station—former passenger station restored in 2004 and now the site for
special events such as weddings, receptions, dinners, etc.

Photos by Ben J. Butler

Stateline Bar & Grill Restaurant on State Street
Photo by Ben J. Butler

A view of State Street looking west into downtown
Photo by Ben J. Butler

The YWCA located on State Street.

Photo by Ben J. Butler

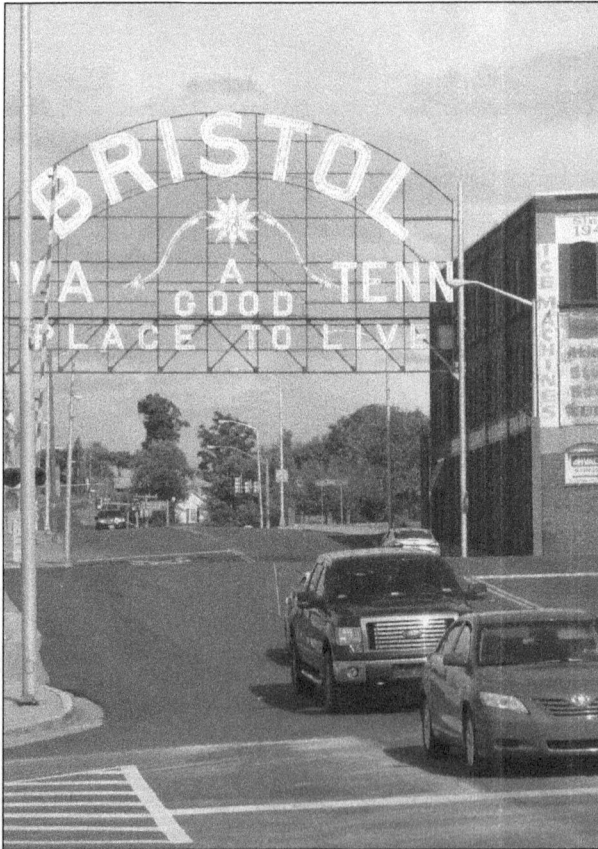

Historic Bristol VA/TN slogan sign which spans State Street near the Train Station.

Photo by Ben J. Butler

About the Author

Dr. Wayne Ballard is a native of Wooster, Ohio, and a graduate of Oklahoma Baptist University with a Bachelor of Arts; Golden Gate Baptist Theological Seminary with a Master of Divinity; Southern Baptist Theological Seminary with a PhD in Old Testament Studies; and University of Tennessee, Knoxville, with a PhD in Higher Education Administration. He is the father of Brack and Zachary Ballard. Brack is a third-year divinity student at Gardner-Webb University. Zach is a senior at Carson-Newman University. A third son, Henderson "Baby Jake" Ballard, died in 2000 at the age of seventeen months.

Wayne is married to Kim Cook Ballard, and they make their home in Strawberry Plains, Tennessee. He is a tenured faculty member at Carson-Newman University, where he has served for the past twelve years as Associate Professor of Religion. He also served as Assistant Professor of Religion at Campbell University in North Carolina. He has served on church staffs in various positions in Oklahoma, California, Montana, Indiana, Ohio, North Carolina, Tennessee, and Virginia. He has authored or coauthored seven books and numerous journal articles.

Other available titles from SMYTH& HELWYS®

#Connect
Reaching Youth Across the Digital Divide
Brian Foreman

Reaching our youth across the digital divide is a struggle for parents, ministers, and other adults who work with Generation Z—today's teenagers. *#Connect* leads readers into the technological landscape, encourages conversations with teenagers, and reminds us all to be the presence of Christ in every facet of our lives.   *978-1-57312-693-9 120 pages/pb* **$13.00**

Beginnings
A Reverend and a Rabbi Talk About the Stories of Genesis
Michael Smith and Rami Shapiro

Editor Aaron Herschel Shapiro declares that stories "must be retold—not just repeated, but reinvented, reimagined, and reexperienced" to remain vital in the world. Mike and Rami continue their conversations from the *Mount and Mountain* books, exploring the places where their traditions intersect and diverge, listening to each other as they respond to the stories of Genesis.   *978-1-57312-772-1 202 pages/pb* **$18.00**

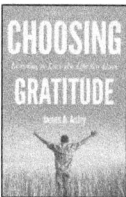

Choosing Gratitude
Learning to Love the Life You Have
James A. Autry

Autry reminds us that gratitude is a choice, a spiritual—not social—process. He suggests that if we cultivate gratitude as a way of being, we may not change the world and its ills, but we can change our response to the world. If we fill our lives with moments of gratitude, we will indeed love the life we have.   *978-1-57312-614-4 144 pages/pb* **$15.00**

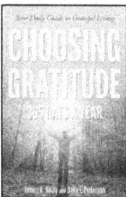

Choosing Gratitude 365 Days a Year
Your Daily Guide to Grateful Living
James A. Autry and Sally J. Pederson

Filled with quotes, poems, and the inspired voices of both Pederson and Autry, in a society consumed by fears of not having "enough"—money, possessions, security, and so on—this book suggests that if we cultivate gratitude as a way of being, we may not change the world and its ills, but we can change our response to the world.   *978-1-57312-689-2 210 pages/pb* **$18.00**

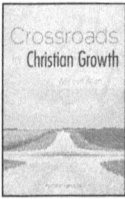

Crossroads in Christian Growth
W. Loyd Allen

Authentic Christian life presents spiritual crises and we struggle to find a hero walking with God at a crossroads. With wisdom and sincerity, W. Loyd Allen presents Jesus as our example and these crises as stages in the journey of growth we each take toward maturity in Christ.   *978-1-57312-753-0 164 pages/pb* **$15.00**

A Divine Duet
Ministry and Motherhood
Alicia Davis Porterfield, ed.

Each essay in this inspiring collection is as different as the mother-minister who wrote it, from theologians to chaplains, inner-city ministers to rural-poverty ministers, youth pastors to preachers, mothers who have adopted, birthed, and done both.   *978-1-57312-676-2 146 pages/pb* **$16.00**

The Exile and Beyond (All the Bible series)
Wayne Ballard

The Exile and Beyond brings to life the sacred literature of Israel and Judah that comprises the exilic and postexilic communities of faith. It covers Ezekiel, Isaiah, Haggai, Zechariah, Malachi, 1 & 2 Chronicles, Ezra, Nehemiah, Joel, Jonah, Song of Songs, Esther, and Daniel.   *978-1-57312-759-2 196 pages/pb* **$16.00**

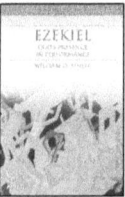

Ezekiel (Smyth & Helwys Annual Bible Study series)
God's Presence in Performance
William D. Shiell

Through a four-session Bible study for individuals and groups, Shiell interprets the book of Ezekiel as a four-act drama to be told to those living out their faith in a strange, new place. Shiell encourages congregations to listen to God's call, accept where God has planted them, surrender the shame of their past, receive a new heart from God, and allow God to breathe new life into them.   *Teaching Guide 978-1-57312-755-4 192 pages/pb* **$14.00**
Study Guide 978-1-57312-756-1 126 pages/pb **$6.00**

Fierce Love
Desperate Measures for Desperate Times
Jeanie Miley

Fierce Love is about learning to see yourself and know yourself as a conduit of love, operating from a full heart instead of trying to find someone to whom you can hook up your emotional hose and fill up your empty heart.   *978-1-57312-810-0 276 pages/pb* **$18.00**

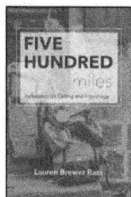

Five Hundred Miles
Reflections on Calling and Pilgrimage
Lauren Brewer Bass

Spain's Camino de Santiago, the Way of St. James, has been a
cherished pilgrimage path for centuries, visited by countless people
searching for healing, solace, purpose, and hope. These stories from
her five-hundred-mile-walk is Lauren Brewer Bass's honest look at the often wind-
ing, always surprising journey of a calling.   *978-1-57312-812-4 142 pages/pb* **$16.00**

Galatians (Smyth & Helwys Bible Commentary)
Marion L. Soards and Darrell J. Pursiful

In Galatians, Paul endeavored to prevent the Gentile converts from
embracing a version of the gospel that insisted on their observance
of a form of the Mosaic Law. He saw with a unique clarity that such
a message reduced the crucified Christ to being a mere agent of the
Law. For Paul, the gospel of Jesus Christ alone, and him crucified,
had no place in it for the claim that Law-observance was necessary for believers to
experience the power of God's grace.   *978-1-57312-771-4 384 pages/hc* **$55.00**

God's Servants the Prophets
Bryan Bibb

God's Servants, the Prophets covers the Israelite and Judean prophetic
literature from the preexilic period. It includes Amos, Hosea, Isaiah,
Micah, Zephaniah, Nahum, Habakkuk, Jeremiah, and Obadiah.
          978-1-57312-758-5 208 pages/pb **$16.00**

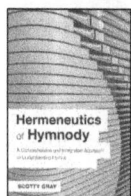

Hermeneutics of Hymnody
A Comprehensive and Integrated Approach to Understanding Hymns
Scotty Gray

Scotty Gray's *Hermeneutics of Hymnody* is a comprehensive and
integrated approach to understanding hymns. It is unique in its
holistic and interrelated exploration of seven of the broad facets
of this most basic forms of Christian literature. A chapter is devoted to each and
relates that facet to all of the others.   *978-157312-767-7 432 pages/pb* **$28.00**

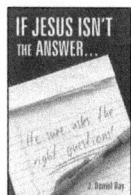

If Jesus Isn't the Answer . . . He Sure Asks the Right Questions!
J. Daniel Day

Taking eleven of Jesus' questions as its core, Day invites readers
into their own conversation with Jesus. Equal parts testimony,
theological instruction, pastoral counseling, and autobiography,
the book is ultimately an invitation to honest Christian discipleship.
          978-1-57312-797-4 148 pages/pb **$16.00**

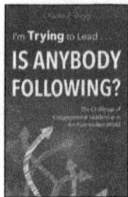

I'm Trying to Lead . . . Is Anybody Following?
The Challenge of Congregational Leadership in the
Postmodern World

Charles B. Bugg

Bugg provides us with a view of leadership that has theological integrity, honors the diversity of church members, and reinforces the brave hearts of church leaders who offer vision and take risks in the service of Christ and the church. *978-1-57312-731-8 136 pages/pb* **$13.00**

James M. Dunn and Soul Freedom
Aaron Douglas Weaver

James Milton Dunn, over the last fifty years, has been the most aggressive Baptist proponent for religious liberty in the US. Soul freedom—voluntary, uncoerced faith and an unfettered individual conscience before God—is the basis of his understanding of church-state separation and the historic Baptist basis of religious liberty.

978-1-57312-590-1 224 pages/pb **$18.00**

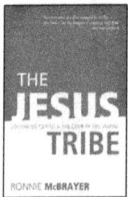

The Jesus Tribe
Following Christ in the Land of the Empire

Ronnie McBrayer

The Jesus Tribe fleshes out the implications, possibilities, contradictions, and complexities of what it means to live within the Jesus Tribe and in the shadow of the American Empire.

978-1-57312-592-5 208 pages/pb **$17.00**

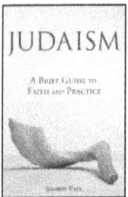

Judaism
A Brief Guide to Faith and Practice

Sharon Pace

Sharon Pace's newest book is a sensitive and comprehensive introduction to Judaism. How does belief in the One God and a universal morality shape the way in which Jews see the world? How does one find meaning in life and the courage to endure suffering? How does one mark joy and forge community ties? *978-1-57312-644-1 144 pages/pb* **$16.00**

Looking Around for God
The Strangely Reverent Observations of an Unconventional Christian

James A. Autry

Looking Around for God, Autry's tenth book, is in many ways his most personal. In it he considers his unique life of faith and belief in God. Autry is a former Fortune 500 executive, author, poet, and consultant whose work has had a significant influence on leadership thinking.

978-157312-484-3 144 pages/pb **$16.00**

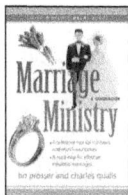

Marriage Ministry: A Guidebook
Bo Prosser and Charles Qualls

This book is equally helpful for ministers, for nearly/newlywed couples, and for thousands of couples across our land looking for fresh air in their marriages. *1-57312-432-X 160 pages/pb* **$16.00**

Meeting Jesus Today
For the Cautious, the Curious, and the Committed
Jeanie Miley

Meeting Jesus Today, ideal for both individual study and small groups, is intended to be used as a workbook. It is designed to move readers from studying the Scriptures and ideas within the chapters to recording their journey with the Living Christ.

978-1-57312-677-9 320 pages/pb **$19.00**

The Ministry Life
101 Tips for Ministers' Spouses
John and Anne Killinger

While no pastor does his or her work alone, roles for a spouse or partner are much more flexible and fluid now than they once were. Spouses who want to support their minister-mates' vocation may wonder where to begin. Whatever your talents may be, the Killingers have identified a way to put those gifts to work. *978-1-57312-769-1 252 pages/pb* **$19.00**

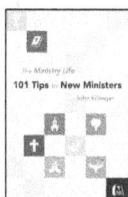

The Ministry Life
101 Tips for New Ministers
John Killinger

Sharing years of wisdom from more than fifty years in ministry and teaching, *The Ministry Life: 101 Tips for New Ministers* by John Killinger is filled with practical advice and wisdom for a minister's day-to-day tasks as well as advice on intellectual and spiritual habits to keep ministers of any age healthy and fulfilled. *978-1-57312 662-5 244 pages/pb* **$19.00**

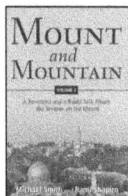

Mount and Mountain
Vol. 2: A Reverend and a Rabbi Talk About the Sermon on the Mount
Rami Shapiro and Michael Smith

This book, focused on the Sermon on the Mount, represents the second half of Mike and Rami's dialogue. In it, Mike and Rami explore the text of Jesus' sermon cooperatively, contributing perspectives drawn from their lives and religious traditions and seeking moments of illumination. *978-1-57312-654-0 254 pages/pb* **$19.00**

Of Mice and Ministers
Musings and Conversations About Life, Death, Grace, and Everything
Bert Montgomery

With stories about pains, joys, and everyday life, *Of Mice and Ministers* finds Jesus in some unlikely places and challenges us to do the same. From tattooed women ministers to saying the "N"-word to the brotherly kiss, Bert Montgomery takes seriously the lesson from Psalm 139— where can one go that God is not already there?   *978-1-57312-733-2 154 pages/pb* **$14.00**

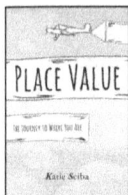

Place Value
The Journey to Where You Are
Katie Sciba

Does a place have value? Can a place change us? Is it possible for God to use the place you are in to form you? From Victoria, Texas to Indonesia, Belize, Australia, and beyond, Katie Sciba's wanderlust serves as a framework to understand your own places of deep emotion and how God may have been weaving redemption around you all along.

978-157312-829-2 138 pages/pb **$15.00**

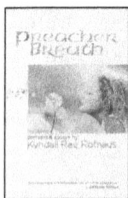

Preacher Breath
Sermon & Essays
Kyndall Rae Rothaus

"*Preacher Breath* is a worthy guide, leading the reader room by room with wisdom, depth, and a spiritual maturity far beyond her years, so that the preaching house becomes a holy, joyful home. . . . This book is soul kindle for a preacher's heart."   —Danielle Shroyer
Pastor, Author of *The Boundary-Breaking* God
978-1-57312-734-9 208 pages/pb **$16.00**

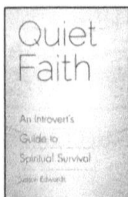

Quiet Faith
An Introvert's Guide to Spiritual Survival
Judson Edwards

In eight finely crafted chapters, Edwards looks at key issues like evangelism, interpreting the Bible, dealing with doubt, and surviving the church from the perspective of a confirmed, but sometimes reluctant, introvert. In the process, he offers some provocative insights that introverts will find helpful and reassuring.   *978-1-57312-681-6 144 pages/pb* **$15.00**

Reading Deuteronomy
(Reading the Old Testament series)
A Literary and Theological Commentary
Stephen L. Cook

A lost treasure for large segments of today's world, the book of Deuteronomy stirs deep longing for God and moves readers to a place of intimacy with divine otherness, holism, and will for person-centered community. The consistently theological interpretation reveals the centrality of this book for faith. 978-1-57312-757-8 *286 pages/pb* **$22.00**

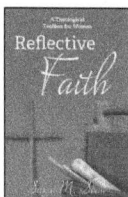

Reflective Faith
A Theological Toolbox for Women
Susan M. Shaw

In *Reflective Faith*, Susan Shaw offers a set of tools to explore difficult issues of biblical interpretation, theology, church history, and ethics—especially as they relate to women. Reflective faith invites intellectual struggle and embraces the unknown; it is a way of discipleship, a way to love God with your mind, as well as your heart, your soul, and your strength. 978-1-57312-719-6 *292 pages/pb* **$24.00**

Workbook 978-1-57312-754-7 *164 pages/pb* **$12.00**

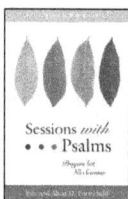

Sessions with Psalms (Sessions Bible Studies series)
Prayers for All Seasons
Eric and Alicia D. Porterfield

Useful to seminar leaders during preparation and group discussion, as well as in individual Bible study, *Sessions with Psalms* is a ten-session study designed to explore what it looks like for the words of the psalms to become the words of our prayers. Each session is followed by a thought-provoking page of questions. 978-1-57312-768-4 *136 pages/pb* **$14.00**

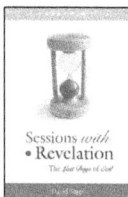

Sessions with Revelation
(Sessions Bible Studies series)
The Final Days of Evil
David Sapp

David Sapp's careful guide through Revelation demonstrates that it is a letter of hope for believers; it is less about the last days of history than it is about the last days of evil. Without eliminating its mystery, Sapp unlocks Revelation's central truths so that its relevance becomes clear.

978-1-57312-706-6 *166 pages/pb* **$14.00**

To order call **1-800-747-3016** or visit **www.helwys.com**

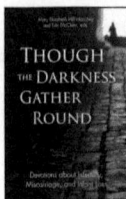

Though the Darkness Gather Round
Devotions about Infertility, Miscarriage, and Infant Loss
Mary Elizabeth Hill Hanchey and Erin McClain, eds.

Much courage is required to weather the long grief of infertility and the sudden grief of miscarriage and infant loss. This collection of devotions by men and women, ministers, chaplains, and lay leaders who can speak of such sorrow, is a much-needed resource and precious gift for families on this journey and the faith communities that walk beside them.

978-1-57312-811-7 180 pages/pb **$19.00**

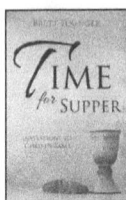

Time for Supper
Invitations to Christ's Table
Brett Younger

Some scholars suggest that every meal in literature is a communion scene. Could every meal in the Bible be a communion text? Could every passage be an invitation to God's grace? These meditations on the Lord's Supper help us listen to the myriad of ways God invites us to gratefully, reverently, and joyfully share the cup of Christ. 978-1-57312-720-2 246 pages/pb **$18.00**

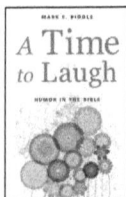

A Time to Laugh
Humor in the Bible
Mark E. Biddle

With characteristic liveliness, Mark E. Biddle explores the ways humor was intentionally incorporated into Scripture. Drawing on Biddle's command of Hebrew language and cultural subtleties, A *Time to Laugh* guides the reader through the stories of six biblical characters who did rather unexpected things. 978-1-57312-683-0 164 pages/pb **$14.00**

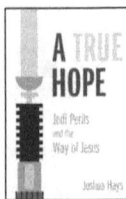

A True Hope
Jedi Perils and the Way of Jesus
Joshua Hays

Star Wars offers an accessible starting point for considering substantive issues of faith, philosophy, and ethics. In A *True Hope*, Joshua Hays explores some of these challenging ideas through the sayings of the Jedi Masters, examining the ways the worldview of the Jedi is at odds with that of the Bible. 978-1-57312-770-7 186 pages/pb **$18.00**

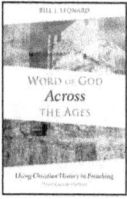

Word of God Across the Ages
Using Christian History in Preaching
Bill J. Leonard

In this third, enlarged edition, Bill J. Leonard returns to the roots of the Christian story to find in the lives of our faithful forebears examples of the potent presence of the gospel. Through these stories, those who preach today will be challenged and inspired as they pursue the divine Word in human history through the ages.   *978-1-57312-828-5 174 pages/pb* **$19.00**

The World Is Waiting for You
Celebrating the 50th Ordination Anniversary of Addie Davis
Pamela R. Durso & LeAnn Gunter Johns, eds.

Hope for the church and the world is alive and well in the words of these gifted women. Keen insight, delightful observations, profound courage, and a gift for communicating the good news are woven throughout these sermons. The Spirit so evident in Addie's calling clearly continues in her legacy.   *978-1-57312-732-5 224 pages/pb* **$18.00**

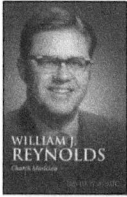

William J. Reynolds
Church Musician
David W. Music

William J. Reynolds is renowned among Baptist musicians, music ministers, song leaders, and hymnody students. In eminently readable style, David W. Music's comprehensive biography describes Reynolds's family and educational background, his career as a minister of music, denominational leader, and seminary professor.   *978-1-57312-690-8 358 pages/pb* **$23.00**

With Us in the Wilderness
Finding God's Story in Our Lives
Laura A. Barclay

What stories compose your spiritual biography? In *With Us in the Wilderness*, Laura Barclay shares her own stories of the intersection of the divine and the everyday, guiding readers toward identifying and embracing God's presence in their own narratives.

978-1-57312-721-9 120 pages/pb **$13.00**

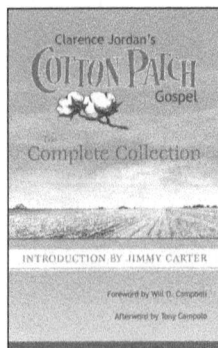

www.ingramcontent.com/pod-product-compliance
Lightning Source LLC
Chambersburg PA
CBHW072349090426
42741CB00012B/2978